PRIDE OF BRITAIN

PRIDE OF BRITAIN

Kirsteen Lupton and Family
With Jeff Hudson

Published by Virgin Books 2008

This book is a work of non-fiction based on the life, experiences and
recollections of the author. The author has stated to the publishers that
the contents of this book are true.

The title 'Pride of Britain' is used with the kind permission of MGN Limited

First published in Great Britain in 2008 by
Virgin Books
Random House
20 Vauxhall Bridge Road
London SW1V 2SA

www.virginbooks.com
www.rbooks.co.uk

Addresses for companies within The Random House Group Limited
can be found at: www.randomhouse.co.uk/offices.htm

The Random House Group Limited Reg. No. 954009

A CIP catalogue record for this book is available from the British Library

ISBN 9781905264315

The Random House Group Limited supports The Forest Stewardship
Council [FSC], the leading international forest certification organisation.
All our titles that are printed on Greenpeace approved FSC certified paper
carry the FSC logo.
Our paper procurement policy can be found at www.rbooks.co.uk/environment

Mixed Sources
Product group from well-managed
forests and other controlled sources
www.fsc.org Cert no. TT-COC-2139
© 1996 Forest Stewardship Council
FSC

Typeset by TW Typesetting, Plymouth, Devon
Printed and bound in the UK by
CPI Mackays, Chatham ME5 8TD

2 4 6 8 10 9 7 5 3 1

This book is dedicated to the staff of
Great Ormond Street Hospital for Children

AUTHOR'S NOTE
This book is written by me and my family. Without them
I wouldn't be alive today. Because I was so young,
I don't know a lot of the details about what was wrong
with me. I thought it would be best if they told the
stories themselves.

Contents

Foreword

I first met Kirsteen in 2006 when, quite rightly, she was awarded a Daily Mirror Pride of Britain award.

Why was she there? Simply because she is an extraordinary young woman, beautiful without, and beautiful within. Some are born 'special' through privilege. Some are 'special' because they have an innate talent. Kirsteen is 'special' because of her spirit. This book is her latest venture to raise money to help other children who have suffered physically, like her, and who have spent endless years in and out of hospital. Her story is inspirational. Take time to read it; I believe it will perhaps make you see the world in a different way, bring more kindness into your life, and bring smiles and sunshine on even the bleakest day.

On October 27, 1993, Kirsteen Lupton was born in Glasgow to Jill and Martin Lupton. Born with her bladder outside her body, Kirsteen was just a few hours old when she underwent emergency surgery. A day of joy had turned into one of fear and helplessness. It would not be the last.

Through the years, Jill and Martin have been regular visitors to hospital, as Kirsteen has endured numerous operations. They have watched their little girl live with terrible pain, not knowing what to do for the best, listening to her cries. Theirs is a story of courage and pride, as they have watched their very ill daughter grow into a stunning young woman. Over the years, Kirsteen has been looked after by the staff at Great Ormond Street Hospital in London. As she grew, she became determined to raise money for the hospital. To do this, she has given some very brave speeches, modelled at a fashion show, arranged for the proceeds of her school play to go to the hospital and many other things besides. At one event she raised £20,000 in just ten minutes by auctioning her own signature.

'I would do anything for Great Ormond Street,' she says. 'Because I've grown up seeing so many sick children, it makes me stronger to help raise money as a thank you to the hospital. I want to be a doctor and would love to work there.'

Kirsteen will have to use a catheter for the rest of her life, but her spirit remains undaunted. The day I met her she was busy charming a room full of people. As she received her Pride of Britain award, she spoke so beautifully of those who have helped her. Movie star Jude Law fell in love with her, saying she gave hope and inspiration to everyone. McFly, the band of the moment, gave her a signed guitar and the then-Prime Minister Tony Blair invited her to Downing Street the next day. Now that was a great day for any girl.

I believe that Kirsteen has an outstanding future ahead of her. She is special because of the devotion of her family and her courage. Through it all, she gives so many others hope. She makes the difference and I wish her every happiness in the world.

Carol Vorderman

2008

Prologue: Save Me

KIRSTEEN LUPTON: 'Save me! Save me! Don't let them kill me!'

I was seven years old when I screamed those words.

Seven years old and terrified. I looked desperately up at Mum and Dad from my hospital bed. They were crying too. I wanted them to reach out and pick me up and make it all right. I wanted them to cuddle me – anything to stop the doctors taking me away.

'Help me!'

But it didn't matter how loudly I screamed. They couldn't cuddle me. There was nothing they could do as I was wheeled towards the operating theatre. I weighed one and a half stone, I hadn't eaten for four weeks and if I didn't have this operation I could be dead within days.

But you don't think rationally when you're ill.

'Please! Mummy, Daddy – save me!'

I heard their voices. They kept saying, 'It's going to be all right, don't worry, Kirsteen. It's going to be all right.' But I wasn't listening. I was too scared.

And I wasn't the only one.

Two nurses were watching as my bed was pushed away. I looked helplessly up at them but they couldn't look back. They were shaking, holding each other. Both of them were sobbing their hearts out.

That's when it hit me.

'If the nurses are crying – if they're scared – then they must think I might not be coming out.'

Oh God, no!

'Save me! Save me!'

I had to be held down as the anaesthetic was administered. Seconds later I was unconscious.

But I had seen the question in the eyes of the doctors, the nurses and Mum and Dad. The question was – would I ever wake up?

Would I come out of the operating theatre alive?

CHAPTER 1

There's a Problem

KIRSTEEN: I was born on 27 October 1993 in the Queen Mother's Hospital in Glasgow. It should have been the happiest day of my mother's life. She was getting the daughter she'd always wanted. She already had two beautiful boys, Kenneth and Martin Jr, born three and one and a half years earlier, respectively. But something had been bugging Mum all through this pregnancy. Something she couldn't put her finger on.

JILL: Nobody would listen to me. There was no evidence to support it. But I didn't *think* there was something wrong; I *knew*.

I told my husband Martin early on.

'What do you mean?' he asked.

'There's something wrong with this baby. I just know it.'

He tried to reassure me, but I was adamant. With my first two babies I had felt different somehow. I couldn't explain it. It was just a feeling. I've never had one like it before or since. But it was so strong. I just knew.

The next day we went to the Queen Mother's Hospital for another scan. Just like before, the results were fine.

'See,' Martin said. 'There's nothing wrong.'

But I knew otherwise. We went for five scans in total: the usual two, then two more when I expressed my fears and another the day before I gave birth. I even had a procedure called an amniocentesis to test for Down's syndrome, spina bifida or some other genetic abnormality. It's not a nice experience. The doctor puts a long needle through your tummy and draws off some of the amniotic fluid that surrounds your baby. There are other downsides too: there's a slightly increased risk of miscarriage; and it also takes two or three weeks for the tests to come back. My results came back clear, though. Another tick in the box marked 'Normal'.

But still I wasn't convinced.

One thing we did learn from the scans, though, was the gender of the baby. 'You're having a lovely, healthy little girl, Mrs Lupton,' I was told, although I didn't have too much faith in that either. When I was expecting our second child I asked if they were able to tell us the baby's sex. It was just for practical reasons, really, because I wanted to know whether or not young Kenneth's old clothes would do or whether we had to buy some new little outfits.

With a big smile on his face the doctor told us, 'I'm ninety-seven per cent certain you're having a little girl.'

Oh, that's nice, I thought. One of each. And, of course, it gave me an excuse to go shopping.

But when we left the hospital Martin said he wasn't convinced. 'I can't put it into words,' he said. 'I don't have any reason for it but I just feel there's another little boy in there.'

And when Martin Jr popped out four months later, he was proved right.

Everyone pooh-poohed my worries about the third baby, especially my mother.

'Don't be so stupid,' she snapped. 'You've had all the tests and they've picked up nothing. We'll hear no more of this silly talk.'

But I knew.

MARTIN: When Jill went into labour with Kenneth, our first little boy, the midwife became concerned about the baby's health. 'He's getting too distressed to come out naturally,' she told us. 'We're going to have to bring in the doctors.'

She made a phone call, and a short while later Jill was being wheeled into an operating theatre for an emergency Caesarean section. We were assured that it was a perfectly normal procedure, but everything about it felt very abnormal to me.

I was allowed into theatre with Jill, but I had to get changed into blue surgical 'scrubs'. And whereas we only had one midwife with us before, suddenly there were about a dozen people in the room.

And there were so many lights and machines it looked like a scene from Star Trek.

Exactly the same thing happened when Jill went into labour with our second child and, once again, she was rushed into theatre.

So when Jill fell pregnant for a third time the doctors told us, 'There'll be no risks taken with this one. Your baby will be born by C-section – no argument.' So at least this time we knew what to expect.

'But,' he went on, 'nobody should have more than three Caesareans. The body can't withstand it, so you should consider this your last child.'

That was fine by me and I think Jill's instincts were the same. We'd never really discussed it before then, but I'd always felt that two or three children would be just about perfect. So when it was spelled out to us like this it seemed perfectly all right.

The night before Kirsteen was born I dropped Jill off at the Queen Mother's and helped her to settle in. She felt most uncomfortable being there and let me know it.

'What am I doing here?' she complained. 'I feel such a fraud. I'm not even ill.'

She couldn't see the point of taking a bed from someone who might really need it. But that's Jill all over.

The boys were at Jill's parents in Old Kirkpatrick that night so that's where I headed. Kenneth was three at the time and Martin Jr was one and a half, and although they weren't entirely sure what was going on, they were excited at the prospect of getting a little sister. The main thing, as far as I was concerned, was to make sure they didn't feel left out.

We had dinner and then the boys were allowed to stay up later than usual to play in front of the television as a special treat. I didn't pay much attention to what was on the screen because I was chatting to my in-laws and trying to keep the boys out of mischief. But I suddenly became aware that what was showing was a documentary about childbirth.

We turned up the sound and then sat there mesmerised for a few minutes. The programme was about a condition that caused babies to be born with some of their organs on the outside of the body; the doctors said they did not know its cause, but that it was becoming more common. I'd never seen anything like it. The programme was quite graphic and I found watching all these poor babies being treated very upsetting. I gave it a few minutes then had to switch channels quickly. It really wasn't the sort of thing the boys should be exposed to. And it definitely wasn't something I wanted to be watching the night before my wife gave birth to our daughter.

JILL: It's hard to sleep in hospital, especially when you're thirty-eight weeks gone, so I was up nice and early on the morning of the planned operation. When Martin arrived he filled me in on what the boys were up to, then we got ready to go down.

It was odd knowing that we were going into theatre. When you have a baby naturally you don't have a clue when or how things are going to happen, but you assume that you'll be in bed, not on an operating table. Then, when they do start to happen, you just have to sit back and wait till it's all over. You don't normally get a chance to worry.

The previous two Caesareans hadn't been planned at all but we had got through them, and they were good experience for this one. We were more excited than nervous. I suppose you could say we were even a little blasé. Can you blame us? I had a history of two lovely pregnancies and two fairly straightforward operations, and this one looked like being the same. So if I didn't actually say it, I was certainly thinking, 'Oh, I know what I'm doing – this is easy.' I was so confident. I even remember thinking, 'Well, I hope I'm out in time for Hallowe'en night for the boys.' That was my main concern. We knew we were going to have a wee girl and we knew our way around a C-section. I felt there was nothing that could surprise us now.

Even my underlying belief that something was wrong didn't trouble me unduly at this point. I know that sounds odd, but I'd got used to feeling that there was a problem. I'd dealt with all those emotions weeks before. There was nothing I could do about it now. It was in fate's hands. We all were.

There was nothing to do but wait.

MARTIN: The operating theatre at the Queen Mother's felt like familiar territory by now. Jill didn't seem worried and I certainly wasn't. I hadn't given a second's thought to her predictions – if I'm honest I thought her hormones had been getting the better of her. I'd even been a little bit scornful in the car on the way over to the hospital the day before when she had mentioned it again. 'For God's sake,' I told her, 'stop it. You've had all the tests. Everything's fine.'

The nurses in the theatre did as much as they could to put us at ease while they fixed up the surgical screen across Jill's middle and the anaesthetist went to work. I wasn't going to be able to see anything until they were finished. This was standard practice, of course, although as a policeman I've seen more than my share of blood.

I took my 'usual' seat by Jill's shoulder and we waited for the process to begin. As far as I was concerned, everything had been fine during the pregnancy, it was fine now and it was going to remain that way.

It's odd seeing so many people in surgical gowns peering over your wife's body, all very busy, focused on their jobs. My role was simply to assure Jill that everything was all right. I don't know if she was listening but she seemed remarkably calm. If anything, I was the one who was beginning to feel a little anxious. But, I told myself, we were in good hands.

Kirsteen's delivery was very straightforward. I remember looking at my watch. It was eleven o'clock. Bang on schedule.

Now was the time to be excited. I watched as they lifted the baby from Jill and above the screen to where we could see her. Jill and I exchanged glances that said, 'We've done it!'

I'll never forget that moment. The wee mite was covered in blood and there was a large swirl of umbilical cord around the abdominal area, but she was the most beautiful little girl I'd ever seen. And in a few minutes I'd be able to hold her in my arms and tell her that myself.

As a man watching a birth, you can feel very left out. All eyes are on the mother and then the baby. If the father disappeared in a puff of smoke halfway through, I don't think anyone would raise an eyebrow.

As soon as the baby comes out, the surgeons show him or her to the parents then whisk the little one off to a table where they run through all sorts of tests. Kenneth had a touch of jaundice when he was born, which, along with various other things, can be picked up within seconds. Babies delivered via C-section also need to have their muscles massaged a little because they've bypassed the stretching that usually occurs in natural childbirth.

But this is the point at which it pays to be the partner during a Caesarean, because Dad gets to watch all of this. He sees up close the first moments of life, the first gulps of air of the new arrival. And while the mother is still being stitched, he can give the baby the cuddle he's waited nine months for. That's how it was with Kenneth. That's how it was with Martin Jr.

I got up to watch as they cleaned Kirsteen and ran

through all the usual tests. I'd seen the routine twice before and I knew this was where I could join in. But as I followed my little baby girl over to the table, one of the doctors turned towards me and held me back.

'Why don't you sit down and wait with your wife, sir?' he said, and without questioning it I did.

Jill was still being stitched at the time. I shrugged as I approached her and told her they'd asked me to hold fire. 'Some new procedure,' I said.

Jill said nothing, and as we waited in silence we both tried to catch a glimpse of our little girl, surrounded as she was by a group of five medics.

The minutes passed so slowly. But soon a young doctor left the group and approached us. I stood up to meet him.

'Mr Lupton,' he said, 'congratulations. You have a beautiful baby girl.'

I could hardly stop the feeling of pride that was rising inside me. But the doctor managed it.

'Unfortunately,' he went on, 'there's a problem.'

Time stood still for me right there and then. I struggled to take the words in but they made no sense to me. I wasn't expecting them. It was as though the doctor was speaking a foreign language.

I glanced at Jill as the doctor's words echoed around my head. There's a problem.

'What kind of problem?' I finally managed, terrified.

'We think we can see her bladder.'

What do you say to something like that? No words would form in my mouth. I felt so helpless, like I'd been punched in the stomach. Jill and I looked at each other and I felt tears begin to well. Jill was silent too, but seemed unusually calm. It had to be the anaesthetic, I thought.

I desperately tried to make sense of everything. I remembered seeing Kirsteen's stomach when she was lifted out. There had been something on her abdomen that looked a bit like a peeled tangerine. Was that the problem? I remembered thinking it was part of the umbilical cord. But I'd only caught a fleeting glimpse and it had genuinely made no impression on me.

I realised the doctor was still speaking.

'. . . now, we don't know what the ramifications of that are,' he said, 'but the consultant from Yorkhill Hospital will come and speak to you.'

I nodded, but something was niggling me, something at the back of my mind. Why wasn't I more shocked? Then I remembered the TV documentary from the night before.

Do you ever come across contrived coincidences in literature or in film and feel that you've been short-changed, that the writer has been a bit lazy with the plot and that things never happen that way in real life?

Well, it was happening to me. Just one day earlier I had never heard of a child being born with its organs on the outside of its body. Now, not even twenty-four hours later, I was being told it had happened to my own daughter.

I do wonder whether my reaction to the news would have been different if I hadn't seen that documentary. As it was, I was stunned, and the wind was absolutely knocked out of me, but I was somehow keeping a measure of control over my emotions.

I slumped back down in my chair to digest the news. I knew the tears weren't far away.

Jill's prediction came into my mind. How could she have known and yet the scans had not picked anything up?

Out of nowhere I heard a friendly Australian voice. It was the surgeon who had delivered Kirsteen. He and his colleagues were still working on Jill. Taking the baby out is just the first step in a Caesarean. It can take up to an hour before Mum is ready to leave theatre.

'It doesn't look too hard to fix,' he said. 'It just looks like a bit of minor damage to the abdominal wall. There's nothing much to worry about.'

The feeling of relief at that moment was incredible. And that's when the tears finally arrived.

'It's going to be all right,' I told Jill, who still had more control over her feelings than I did. 'They'll sort her out. It's going to be all right.'

I squeezed her hand as I spoke and smiled through the tears, but I don't know if my words were meant more to calm her or me.

JILL: That news from my surgeon was so welcome. Thank goodness, I thought. It must be no big deal.

But then a few minutes later he let himself down in my eyes when, having just put our minds at rest about Kirsteen's condition, he leaned over and asked, 'Are you sure you want me to go ahead with the sterilisation, seeing as you've got a disabled child?'

Before going in I had been advised to undergo sterilisation after delivery as this would be my third Caesarean, and the maximum doctors recommend. I was expecting it. But there I was, lying helpless on an operating table, having just been told that my baby has a problem. I was utterly confused by what was going on and was being asked this question.

'You have to make up your mind now,' he said. 'Do you want me to go ahead with it or not?'

I said, 'Yes. Of course.'

To me, it made no difference. It wouldn't have altered anything if Kirsteen had been perfectly healthy or if, God forbid, she'd died. I wasn't having three children for the sake of it. I didn't want any more. My body probably couldn't handle it. But what right did this man have speaking to me like that? His insensitivity made me feel worse somehow than the news about Kirsteen. At least that sounded as though it was easy to put right.

How wrong I was.

I was still being seen to when a new figure stepped into the operating theatre. Martin saw him first. It was obvious he was important from the way the other doctors and surgeons greeted him. He came over and introduced himself to us as Mr Alasdair Fyfe, consultant from Yorkhill Hospital. (Yorkhill and the Queen Mother's are joined to each other by a link corridor.)

He wasted no time in getting to the point. I think he was used to people hanging on his every word. And, to be honest, anything he had to say we wanted to hear.

The first thing he said was that Kirsteen had a condition called 'bladder exstrophy'. This occurs when a pelvic bone fails to set properly, allowing the bladder to form outside the body. But he also added some good news, and told us, 'What I can say to you from the outset is, it's not life-threatening.'

Our relief at this point was palpable, only he wasn't finished.

'But you have to understand this: of all the conditions it is possible to do something with, this is the most surgically challenging.' He was looking at us closely now. 'Every case is different but your daughter will never be naturally continent, she'll never have a working bladder she's got control of. She'll never have a normal life.'

My heart sank with these words. And then he dropped the bombshell.

'She's going to face an awful lot of operations over the next few years. The first procedure will be a fairly lengthy process to enclose her bladder. And I want to do it today.'

I couldn't believe it. Our little girl – who we hadn't even touched yet – was going to have an operation. She was less than one hour old and she was being taken from us.

The emotions that I'd managed to keep in check so far came flooding to the surface. If Martin hadn't been there I don't know what I would have done. I was screaming and sobbing and crying out for Kirsteen.

'Oh that poor wee baby. My poor little girl!'

MARTIN: As a policeman, I've seen a lot of horrible things. I'm probably a bit more matter-of-fact about difficult situations than a lot of people because that's what regular exposure to unpleasantness does to you. But when something like this happens to you, when it's brought to your own doorstep, it's another story.

I felt like a child again. I didn't know what to do. I was horrified, numbed, sad. And fearful. What was going to happen to my little girl? A gamut of emotions swirled around inside my head. But worst of all was the uncertainty.

Everyone seemed to be saying something different. Jill and I were so confused, not knowing who or what to believe.

I felt so drained, so washed out with the shock of it all.

JILL: Whatever else I felt then, I wasn't surprised. This was my third Caesarean. I knew how they worked. The doctors lift the baby out, show it to the parents and say things like, 'Isn't he lovely' or 'What a beautiful baby girl'. But they didn't say anything about Kirsteen. They just whisked her away.

Then when they sent Martin back and didn't bundle the baby up for him to hold as usual I got really suspicious.

But still, I wasn't surprised. For weeks I'd been saying that something was wrong. I'd sensed it.

I just hadn't known what.

CHAPTER 2

Was It Something I Did?

KIRSTEEN: I can't imagine what a shock it must have been for Mum and Dad when I arrived. Especially Dad. But even though Mum says she had known that something was wrong, she hadn't known what it was, so she couldn't really prepare herself. Just because she wasn't surprised, that didn't mean she wasn't upset. And when the doctors in the delivery theatre started telling her different stories, it got worse.

JILL: It's one thing expecting bad news. You can prepare yourself so that it's not such a shock. But that's all you can do. It's what happens next that gets to you. It's the fallout, and how you handle that. I didn't know what was going to be wrong with Kirsteen. And I didn't have much more of a clue when it was explained to me after she was born.

All I could think about was this: what caused this problem? How did it happen?

Was it because of me?

I was still lying there in the operating theatre when I first began to wonder. And I couldn't shake the thought. Imagine if it was something that I had done, or not done, or eaten, or not taken. It must have been. There was no other explanation. The smallest mistake when you're pregnant can have devastating effects on the new life in your body. I knew that. Had I been a bit blasé because this was my third? Had I taken unnecessary risks earlier on in the pregnancy? Had I, somehow, caused my little girl to have this problem and put her life in danger.

How could I live with myself now?

What would I say to the wee girl when I was finally allowed to pick her up?

MARTIN: I was in too much of a state of shock to guess what Jill was thinking. I didn't know she was blaming herself, and she didn't mention it to me. At least, not then. We were both too busy worrying about Kirsteen, and I assumed that was why Jill was so quiet. I thought it was fear driving the silence. I didn't realise it was guilt.

I don't think the doctors helped either. They weren't prepared to enter into any kind of discussion with us about what could possibly have caused the problem. I wish they had – it might have put Jill's mind at rest. If she'd have listened, that is.

But they were busy looking after the baby, checking her over, weighing and measuring her, putting her first nappy on, treating the exposed bladder. The last thing on anyone's mind was worrying about Jill and me. And I fully understood that, but we needed more information – something to help us understand what was going on.

One of my most vivid recollections of that time is being kept in the dark. We'd just been hit with the most upsetting news of our lives, yet we were being treated a bit like an audience. I know the doctors and nurses all had jobs to do, and I would have been very disturbed had they not put Kirsteen first, but Jill and I were definitely given the impression that we were in the way.

One thing we were told, however, was Kirsteen's weight. All parents like to know that – it's one of the first things people ask you. 'Is it a boy or a girl? How much does he/she weigh?' And the good news was that Kirsteen was a healthy 6lb 3oz. When they told us that I felt some sort of relief. It somehow seemed to make things a little bit more normal.

Elective Caesareans often produce slightly smaller babies because they are generally delivered before the mother has gone full term, and we were assured that Kirsteen's weight was not an issue. Kenneth had been the lower end of 'normal' when he arrived, and that had been a worry at the time, but in this respect Kirsteen was fine.

I knew Mr Fyfe wanted to get back to Yorkhill as soon as possible, but I couldn't let him leave without hearing some answers.

'Please,' I begged. 'You've got to tell us what's happened to her. Why wasn't it picked up on the scans?'

'We'll have a proper chat later,' Mr Fyfe promised. 'But in basic terms, I can tell you what I think has happened to your daughter.'

He explained to us again what bladder exstrophy actually is. Once again, I remembered seeing what had resembled a wet, peeled tangerine as they lifted her out.

We were told that the condition only presents in one in 50,000 live births, which, although it sounds low in percentage terms, was higher than I would have expected. When you have a scan and you're told there's a one in two million chance of something being wrong, that's OK; the odds are high enough not to be of any real concern. To be honest, you can't imagine that many people. But 50,000 you can. That's a football stadium or a pop concert. We've all seen that many people, and we can all picture a group that size. And it's not that large, really. Not relatively speaking.

According to Mr Fyfe, something goes wrong around the sixth week of pregnancy, but they do not know what, and they certainly don't know how it's triggered.

We learned later that it could have been picked up in the scans. Unfortunately it wasn't a standard feature to be checked at that time. But the clues were there. A full bladder can show up on the scan, and because Kirsteen's bladder was on her outside it never showed as full inside which, apparently, would be treated as suspicious today. If a woman had as many scans now as Jill did then, and each one showed an empty bladder, they would keep scanning until they came across a full one. In our case though, they had assumed it was just an empty bladder.

Having said that, I'm not sure that knowing in advance solves anything beyond preparing you for the emotions you will go through when the baby arrives. There was nothing they could have done medically speaking before the birth, so I'm actually pleased I didn't know until Kirsteen was born. It would have just been worry, worry, worry.

Now that we knew though, I promised myself that I would research the subject as soon as I could. I needed to learn as much as possible about this condition. Whatever could be done for our daughter, I wanted to be aware of it.

But that wasn't the most pressing thing on my mind at that point. As soon as Mr Fyfe disappeared, I just wanted to get out of the operating theatre and be told that I could pick up my wee girl.

And about an hour later that happened.

A nurse came over and told us that Jill was ready to go back to her ward.

Nervously I asked, 'What about Kirsteen?'

'Oh,' she said casually, 'she'll be coming with you.'

It was as if a large load had been lifted from my shoulders. This was what we'd been desperate to hear. Mr Fyfe would be operating on Kirsteen at four o'clock, the nurse said. That gave us nearly four hours to spend with our daughter. Four precious hours.

I stood aside as the nurses pushed Jill's bed out of the room. Right behind her another nurse followed with a tiny white bundle. I knew that inside the mass of blankets and towels was Kirsteen, and I couldn't wait to hold her – but I also knew someone else would have something to say about that.

Even though Jill was still so weak from her operation, no force on Earth was going to stop her having a cuddle with our little girl. She'd waited long enough. We both had.

I watched as the midwife carefully passed the screaming little package over and let her rest on Jill's chest. As soon as the little girl felt her mother's warmth she stopped crying – but that was my cue to start. I thought I'd shed enough tears in the operating theatre. But there were plenty more where they'd come from, it seemed. I could barely see through the tears and Jill was sobbing now, too. We must have looked a complete mess.

But Kirsteen didn't.

Unless you'd been told, you would never have imagined there was anything different about her. To me she looked just wonderful. How could anything be wrong with her? Perhaps the doctors were mistaken?

But who was I fooling? The midwife brought me back to my senses, saying, 'You'll have to be careful with her; she's a fragile little creature. We've taped her bladder up for now, so it shouldn't get in the way. Mr Fyfe will be dealing with that later. She'll need her nappy changed in about an hour, but I'll be popping in and out to help you with that. Now, let's get the wee thing into some clothes.'

As we'd known for some time that we were expecting a little girl, Jill was prepared with lots of pink outfits. I handed the midwife a tiny vest and a cute Babygro. They looked like doll's clothes in my hands.

As soon as she was lifted away from Jill, Kirsteen started crying again, but the midwife was very soothing and tried to be as quick as possible. I watched as the blankets came off Kirsteen. I don't know what I was expecting to see but she looked perfectly normal in her little nappy. There was just an extra bit of padding in place to protect the exposed bladder, but you couldn't see it.

In no time at all, it seemed, the midwife had Kirsteen ready to go back to her mother.

'She's beautiful,' she said. 'Enjoy these moments.'

And then she was gone. I looked around. Apart from me, Jill and the new addition to our family, the room was empty. We were alone at last.

'Are you going to have her all day then?' I asked Jill.

'Just another few minutes, Martin.'

I nodded, smiled and stroked Kirsteen's little head. 'We've done it,' I said. 'She's just beautiful.'

And she was. She had a shock of dark hair and tiny, delicate little features. To this day I can still remember every last detail.

I was determined to make the most of the precious hours we had with her.

JILL: Those first moments holding Kirsteen were so wonderful. I was lying in my awkward hospital bed, but the back of it tilted so that I could, at least, sit up and give her a lovely cuddle. There was nothing of her. She was so tiny, so light. The doctors don't like you to exert yourself after an operation, but to me she weighed nothing and holding her was effortless. Even if she'd weighed sixteen stone though, I'd have found some way of picking her up. The relief of getting my hands on her after all that time surpassed everything.

It was the most natural thing in the world having her on me. I could hear her little breaths and feel her tiny fingers clawing softly into my skin. I didn't know what to look at first. It was so bright in the room that her little eyes were straining to stay open in the light and her face was so colourful, all pink and fresh. And her little nose and mouth and ears were too cute for words. She looked no different from how the boys had. And she definitely didn't look as though she was in any pain.

But I knew that the hours ahead would be horrible for her. I hated myself for putting her through it. I knew in my heart that whatever Mr Fyfe and his team did would be for her good. But you don't want to think of your little girl, not even a day old, going under the knife. No mother would. It's the worst feeling in the world.

I cried every time I thought about it.

'Martin, how can they operate on this tiny little angel? Look, there's nothing to her. It's not right. It's not right,' I said.

Martin tried to distract me. 'Do you think she looks like a Kirsteen?' he asked.

We'd decided on the name a few weeks earlier, but you never really know if it fits until you see the face it will belong to.

I looked down at her little blinking eyes. 'I think she's a perfect Kirsteen,' I said. 'How could she be called anything else?'

Eventually I had to hand her over to Martin. I was tired and desperately wanted to sleep. But I couldn't miss a moment of the few hours we'd been promised with her.

Seeing Martin hold our new daughter gave me a much-needed boost of energy. You can't fake the love he showed for her. He didn't have to say a word. You could see it in his face. He looked so proud and so happy.

But I began to worry about the future. Mr Fyfe had said that Kirsteen's condition wasn't life-threatening. But any operation carries a certain amount of risk. Before I had children I'd worked in the dental profession and knew that it's not always the operation itself that poses the biggest threat – it's the general anaesthetic. It's a dangerous part of any medical procedure. That's why I can never understand people who go under the knife for vanity; you wouldn't catch me risking a general anaesthetic just for the promise of a flatter tummy – not if you paid me.

What if they got the anaesthetic wrong with Kirsteen? She's so small, I thought. It would be all too easy to give her the wrong dose.

Martin could see I was working myself up so he gave me back Kirsteen to hold on to. I couldn't be upset with her in my arms.

'Well, I guess I'd better let people know what's happening,' he said. 'They'll be worried.'

'What will you tell them?' I asked him.

'I don't really know.'

And that was the problem. We needed to let our families and friends have the news, and we knew they'd ask questions. But we didn't have the answers.

I listened as Martin rang his parents. They live down in Liverpool but they said they'd come up as soon as possible to see Kirsteen and help take care of the boys, while Martin was with us in hospital. They were upset and confused. Just like us. Then he rang my mother who promised to tell the boys their little sister had arrived. Finally he called my sister Suzanne. I have two sisters and one brother. Suzanne is the one I'm closest to. She was horrified to hear our news, but said she'd do anything she could to help.

'Actually, I have got a favour,' Martin said. 'I'm going to have to spend more time here than we'd planned – do you think the boys could stay with you for a while until my parents can come up?'

'Of course they can, don't be silly!' Suzanne said. 'I imagine they'll be getting under Mum's feet by now.'

'Well, if they're not they soon will be. I'll drop them round in the morning.'

Hearing about Kenneth and Martin Jr nearly set me off crying again. I worried about how they would react to their new sister.

'What if they hurt Kirsteen when we get home?' I asked Martin.

'Don't worry yourself; you don't know what state she'll be in,' he tried to reassure me.

'Well I know she's going to be a fragile little thing,' I said. 'And you know what boys are like.' But that would have to be a problem for later, I decided. First of all we had this operation to get through.

'Do you think Kirsteen will pull through?' I asked Martin.

'Of course she will, don't be silly.'

Martin said all the right things. But what happened next made us both doubt his words.

MARTIN: It was only two o'clock in the afternoon but I felt like I'd been awake for a week. The whole day had been like a long, exhausting nightmare. I never realised your emotions could take so much out of you. I felt physically drained, even though it was only my mind that had taken a pounding, not my body.

Jill was on the phone to some of her family when a midwife came in. We chatted briefly while she took a quick look at Kirsteen's notes. I assumed that she had come by to tell us about the operation. But I was wrong. She was carrying a Polaroid camera.

'I'd just like to take a quick picture of Kirsteen,' she said.

A chill shot through me.

'What for?' I asked.

'Oh, it's just standard procedure,' she replied.

But I wasn't convinced. I had been in the police force for too long not to recognise a 'company line'. Every instinct in my body told me the midwife was hiding something.

'What will you do with the picture?' I asked.

'It's just for the files,' she said. 'We photograph everyone who is undergoing surgery.' But she could see I was put out and added, 'Mr Lupton, if it's upsetting for you, I don't have to take the picture. It's up to you.'

'Of course you can,' I said. 'I was just worried about what it meant.'

'I can assure you it's par for the course,' she said. 'I wouldn't want you to think it had any other significance.'

I helped arrange Kirsteen in Jill's arms while the photo was taken. The nurse waited for the Polaroid image to reveal itself, then when she was satisfied she left.

'That's not good,' I said to Jill as soon as the nurse was out of earshot. I still had the distinct impression that we were being fobbed off to some extent. Who were they trying to fool? I knew what the picture meant. How could it have anything other than sinister implications for us? The fact that they'd come and taken a photograph couldn't be a positive thing, could it?

Jill was thinking the same thing. 'Oh, Martin, they don't think Kirsteen is going to pull through.'

Jill was sobbing by now. I joined her. Our little girl, our precious little Kirsteen, would be taken away from us in just hours and we weren't at all confident she'd be coming back. Nothing can prepare you for that realisation. And once it's dawned on you, nothing can make it go away.

It seemed like only five minutes later when a nurse came back for Kirsteen.

'That's never four o'clock,' I said. But it wasn't far off.

She went to take Kirsteen from Jill. 'Just a few more minutes,' Jill asked.

'I'm sorry, I need to take her to Yorkhill now. Don't worry, she'll be back before you know it.'

'Well I'm coming with her,' Jill said.

The nurse looked horrified. I knew I had to step in.

'You can't be getting up, you've just had an operation,' I said.

'We can't leave her on her own,' Jill cried.

'She's in the best hands, Mrs Lupton,' the nurse said.

'You stay here and get your rest. Making yourself ill won't help Kirsteen now, will it?'

She was right. But that wasn't what we were worried about. As she carefully lifted Kirsteen into the small incubator trolley ready to push her along the corridor to Yorkhill, Jill and I both thought the same thing.

Would we ever see our daughter again?

CHAPTER 3

Like Something Out of *Battlestar Galactica*

KIRSTEEN: I think Mum and Dad hold things back when they talk to me because they don't want me to feel bad. But as I've got older I've heard more details about the day I was born and what they went through. I've also learned quite a bit from hearing them talk to friends, or through other members of the family. I feel really sorry for them and guilty that I put them through it, even though I know it wasn't my fault. I'd hate that to happen to me. I can't imagine having a baby who is sick.

When you're the person who's ill you don't really have the energy to worry about how other people are feeling. You don't want them to be upset, but there's nothing you can say or do. And I was only a baby when my problems started. I don't know if it was better or worse for me being so small when the doctors first operated on me. All I know for sure is that I was too young to know what was happening to me.

And from what I understand, Mum and Dad didn't feel any more informed.

MARTIN: Watching the nurse leave with Kirsteen was heartbreaking. I followed them to the lift, where I was told to go back to my wife. When I got back to Jill, she was crying.

'I feel so bloody useless stuck here,' she said.

'There's nothing we can do now,' I told her. 'Come on, you need to rest. When Kirsteen comes out, you'll need all your strength to look after her. It's no good to anyone if you make yourself worse.'

She knew I was right but that didn't stop her hurting. And the fact that we were surrounded by other couples with their tiny new arrivals just made it worse.

'It's not fair, is it?' Jill said. 'Why isn't our little girl allowed to be here with us like all these other babies?'

Out of respect for all the families around us, we tried not to make a scene. The last thing we wanted to do was to spoil their happiness with our tears. But it was so difficult. I pulled the curtain around Jill's bed and, protected from the outside world, we cried together.

I felt just as impotent as Jill. Even though I was mobile, what good was it doing me? The Queen Mother's Maternity Hospital is only a few hundred yards away from Yorkhill but at that moment it felt like another country. What was going on over there?

We tried to talk about other things to take our minds off what was worrying us. It didn't really matter what – anything just to change the subject for a while. I told Jill a few stories about work; it was obvious that she wasn't really listening, but I didn't mind. Then she asked after the boys and I reminded her about the arrangements I'd made with her sister. 'We'll stay at your mother's tonight,' I said, 'then I'll drop them off with Suzanne in the morning on my way here.'

'I really miss them,' Jill said, welling up again. 'When are you going to bring them in here?'

'Not until wee Kirsteen's out of the woods; we've discussed that.'

Jill nodded. 'I know. I just want to give them a great big hug.'

'I'll give them one for you, tonight.'

After a while, I had to fling open the curtain again as we'd begun to feel like caged animals. Seeing the smiling faces of happy parents all around us was still difficult, but it was better than feeling like we were in a prison.

I, at least, could get up and walk around, unlike Jill, and after an hour I went down to the reception area and asked if there was any news.

'Not yet, Mr Lupton,' I was told, 'but she's only been gone a short while. I'd give it some time yet.'

I bought two teas from a vending machine on the way back. Over the next four hours I must have drunk another half a dozen, stopping off at the reception each time.

And each time I got the same answer. 'Mr Lupton, we've heard nothing from Yorkhill, but as soon as they call we'll come right out and find you.'

I remember noticing when the clock hit nine.

'That's five hours now,' I said to Jill. 'That's practically half her life.'

For the next thirty or forty minutes we sat in silence, the only noise around us being the sound of babies feeding or sleeping. One little tot was crying. But no one was talking. The other husbands in the ward had been sent home hours before, but I'd been allowed to stay on after visiting time. There was no way they could throw me out now.

'What's taking them so long?' I thought. 'There must be something wrong. Something must have gone wrong.'

I knew Jill was thinking the same thing. It was written all over her face.

Then, at just before ten, a nurse appeared at the end of the bed. I was on my feet immediately.

'Is she all right?' I couldn't get the words out quickly enough.

'Mr Lupton, Mrs Lupton, Kirsteen's fine,' the nurse said. 'We've just had the call from Yorkhill. I don't know the details but she's out of theatre. Mr Lupton, you can go over there, if you want. Your wife should probably get some sleep now anyway.'

Jill exploded. 'There's no way I'm sleeping now!' she told the nurse. 'Not while my little girl is over there.'

Even as she spoke, tears once more beginning to roll down her cheeks, Jill was trying to lift herself up. The nurse ran to stop her but Jill wasn't having any of it. Another nurse came running over but she was told the same thing.

'I'm going to see my daughter.' Jill pulled herself to her feet, threw a dressing gown on and said to me, 'Well, come on then. Give me a hand.'

And a few minutes later I was helping Jill to shuffle along the corridor that linked the two hospitals.

JILL: The nurses looked shocked when I climbed out of bed. But how could I stay there knowing my daughter was on the other side of the hospital wall? Martin knew better than to argue with me. We must have looked a right pair: both of us sniffing, and me leaning on him for support, as we made our way along the corridor to Yorkhill at ten o'clock at night.

When we got over there, Martin explained who we were and we were directed to the right floor. I was so excited, but nervous as well. We didn't know what they'd done to her, and we didn't know if it had worked. I couldn't stop myself fretting. What must the poor little thing be thinking? I wondered. She must be hating us for putting her through all that. I knew it was silly and that she was too young to be thinking anything at all, but that somehow made it worse – knowing that she was so vulnerable. She was depending on her parents to look after her, and look how she'd spent her first day out of the womb.

We were met outside Kirsteen's room by the registrar, a man called Mr Haddock. He told us that the operation had been a success. They'd achieved what they set out to do.

'Why did it take so long?' I asked.

Martin told me not to interrupt, but the registrar smiled. 'It's all right,' he said. I'm sure he was used to distressed parents. 'It's a relatively complicated procedure and that's how long it takes. Mr Fyfe will see you in the morning and discuss everything with you in detail, but I can tell you basically what we've done.'

He explained that they had put Kirsteen's bladder back inside her and grafted the skin over the top. Also an orthopaedic surgeon called Mr Sherlock had cut and reset her pubic bone so that it now covered her bladder. Everything had been physically put back into position, but they had not, as yet, been able to address Kirsteen's 'plumbing', as he called it.

'Now before you go in,' Mr Haddock said, 'I must warn you. Don't be shocked but Kirsteen is wired up to a lot of monitors and she's also being fed intravenously. She looks like something out of *Battlestar Galactica*, but I can assure you it's perfectly normal.'

More than ever, I needed to see my little girl.

Even though I thought I was prepared, I still had to catch my breath as I stepped through the door. Mr Haddock wasn't joking about the wires. Kirsteen was hooked up to countless instruments and machines and there were tubes coming out of every orifice. She looked terrible. Like a little doll surrounded by giant computers.

Also, the registrar had forgotten to mention that Kirsteen was in plaster from the waist down. Her pubic bone needed to be held in place where it had been reset by Mr Sherlock, so her little legs were in plaster, raised at the knee. But that wasn't the worst of it. To ensure that her legs stayed in the right position a metal bar had been wedged between her feet.

I felt terrible for the little creature. What they'd done to her looked inhumane. But, at the same time, it was such a relief to see her breathing. Just seeing that she was alive, watching her little tummy go up and down as she slept, took a huge weight off my mind.

I saw Martin's shoulders slump as well. We'd both been so tense for the last six hours. But looking at her now, in her little perspex cot, wrapped tightly in white hospital blankets, made me so happy. I felt a familiar welling in my eyes. I thought, I can't cry again. I can't have any tears left.

But I did.

I don't know how long we spent in that room, but it felt like only five minutes before a nurse came in and said we'd have to leave for the night.

'Can't we just pull up a chair in here?' I asked.

'I'm sorry, we don't allow overnight visitors unless it's an emergency.'

I felt angry at being thrown out, but thought that it was good news, at least, that the doctors didn't consider Kirsteen to be an emergency. For the first time all day, I allowed myself to think she was going to be all right.

'We're over the worst now, Martin,' I whispered softly.

I had no idea when I said those words how wrong I would turn out to be.

MARTIN: Kirsteen really did look like something from a science-fiction movie. It was impossible not to be upset, seeing her with all those tubes. But we were assured that she was in no pain, and that there was nothing to be served by us being there as they expected her to sleep all through the night.

It was a struggle to get Jill back to the Queen Mother's. But at least she would be staying close by. I had a half-hour drive back to our house in Milngavie, as it was too late by now to see the boys at Jill's parents' house in Old Kirkpatrick.

Before I set off I made sure Jill was settled. The ward sister was not at all pleased that she'd been walking. 'Why they let you up I don't know,' she scolded.

'Remember to give those boys a hug from me,' Jill told me as I kissed her goodbye.

Physically, she was drained, yet I knew mentally she would be up all night thinking.

Thinking and worrying.

The drive that night was the loneliest of my life. Pulling out of Glasgow city centre I could see a few stragglers making their way home after a night out in the clubs and bars. They all looked so happy. They had no idea of what was going on in that imposing building just up the hill.

First thing the next morning I was back at the hospital. I don't think Jill had slept a wink. We had a meeting with Mr Fyfe scheduled for an hour later. Until then, we would be at Kirsteen's bedside.

I pushed Jill in a wheelchair through the hospital link tunnel, wondering why we hadn't used one the night before. It was a lot better for Jill's stitches this way.

My heart sank as we entered Kirsteen's room. I think I'd hoped it was all a bad dream. But there she was: still connected to the National Grid and, worst of all, still encased in that terrible plaster.

I controlled my emotions this time, though. I didn't think I had any more tears to shed, but I think that what really stopped me was the sickening realisation that I had no idea how long she would be like this. For all I knew, we could still be visiting Kirsteen in this intimidating room in six months' time. Only one person could allay my fears.

Mr Fyfe was a small man, but had an air of confidence that was quite reassuring. I felt very comfortable in his company. I can't say he was particularly considerate towards either my or Jill's feelings, but he appeared to know what he was doing, and Kirsteen, we felt, was in very good hands.

He ran through the same things that Mr Haddock, the registrar, had briefed us on the night before, reiterating that the work that had taken place during her operation had tackled the physical problem rather than any of the 'plumbing' arrangements. The bladder was now where it should be, and in the future they would go in again and try to address its functionality.

'I can tell you that we consider last night's operation a success,' Mr Fyfe said. 'But you have to be aware that it is only the first part of our plan for her recovery. We have no choice but to take things slowly. I can't promise you it will be easy, but she will have the best care available.'

Despite the information he gave us, I started to feel as if Mr Fyfe was keeping some things about Kirsteen's condition to himself. I found this frustrating. As a police officer, I'm used to asking questions and getting answers, and while I wouldn't go so far as to say he was dismissive of our concerns, putting us at ease certainly wasn't his priority. He told us we'd be going step by step, but he never really explained it fully. He never let us in on the bigger picture.

Mr Fyfe and his team were mainly worried about protecting Kirsteen's kidneys. They told us that one was perfect, while the other had sustained some degree of damage. The way it was explained to us, the good kidney would continue to develop and take over a greater proportion of the overall kidney function. But the one that was damaged would not grow so fast. In the fullness of time, it would assume less responsibility.

I was satisfied that the Yorkhill team had a plan, even though Jill and I still felt we didn't have the complete picture, but I was distraught when I learned how long term it was to be.

'Kirsteen will need to have an operation called a Mitrofanoff when she is four years old,' Mr Fyfe said.

Four years? For four years she would be suffering in whatever form that took – and we didn't even know at that stage what her capacity for day-to-day living would be.

The Mitrofanoff, Mr Fyfe continued, would involve taking some appendix tissue and using that to make Kirsteen's bladder big and retentive. The kidneys manufacture urine and drain it through the ureters into the bladder. The doctors' worry was that if they didn't do something – and this was where the Mitrofanoff came in – there would be reflux, meaning that the urine would travel back through the ureters and cause damage to the kidneys.

'Well, what do you make of all that?' I asked Jill when we left Mr Fyfe.

'Four years, Martin. That's an awfully long time.'

'And I get the impression that won't be the end of it either.'

'Oh, that poor girl,' Jill said. 'What have we done to her?'

We spent a few hours together at Kirsteen's bedside. There was no change in her condition, and the intravenous feeding meant she wanted for nothing. Nurses came in every hour to change her little nappy. This was made more difficult by the leg plaster, but they managed to make it look fairly straightforward. I tried to take in as much as I could. We both desperately wanted to be involved in Kirsteen's life as soon as possible, and, at the moment, changing her nappy and making sure she was comfortable looked our best bet. I couldn't wait.

I would have gladly stayed there all day, but we both felt I needed to see the boys. I was missing them like mad, but more than that I was positive that Jill's mum would be at her wits' end by now. I needed to get back to her house just to give her a breather.

When I arrived in Old Kirkpatrick I could see that it wasn't just my mother-in-law who was anxious for a break. Little Kenneth made it very clear that he didn't want to spend any more time there. And from the way Martin Jr hugged me, you would have thought I'd been away for a year.

'Don't worry, lads, you'll be going to see your Aunty Suzanne tomorrow,' I told them.

I hadn't announced my plans for the boys to Jill's parents though, and when I mentioned them over lunch, her father, Gilbert, who is a sweet man, nodded in agreement. 'You're welcome to stay here as long as you like,' he said, 'but our place is with Jill in the hospital.' He felt the sooner the boys were off his hands, the more time he could spend with his daughter and new granddaughter.

But Jill's mother, Gay, took a different view. 'You can't do that!' she shouted. The ferocity of her outburst took me by surprise.

'What's the problem?' I asked. 'Suzanne offered. And we don't know how long we're going to be in Yorkhill with Kirsteen. You can't be looking after a three- and a one-and-a-half-year-old.'

'Oh no, that will never do,' she continued, oblivious to my words. 'Young John is revising for his exams. You can't take them there.'

John, Suzanne's eldest boy, was sitting his standard grade prelims at the time.

I said, 'Well, Suzanne's obviously considered that and she's still happy to help. She's a grown woman. She knows what she's doing. And in any case, she's worried about her new little niece and wants to do everything she can to help.'

That didn't cut any ice either.

'All I'm worried about is wee John's exams – that's more important than anything.'

I couldn't believe what I was hearing. I wanted to bite my tongue, but I couldn't. 'So young John's exams are more important than Kirsteen's health?' I asked her bluntly.

'Yes they are!'

Gay and I had never seen eye to eye but I usually managed to keep my opinions to myself for the sake of family harmony and, in particular, out of deference to her husband, whom I admired greatly.

On this occasion, however, I didn't even try to hold back. Half a dozen years of bottled-up resentment came pouring out in Gay's direction. I was shaking with rage.

I gathered the boys' things together as quickly as I could and left the house. They were too young to understand what was going on, but I'm sure they sensed that all was not well, and I felt guilty at having exposed them to the argument.

Suzanne was surprised to see the boys so early, but she happily took them in. I thanked her and explained a little of what had gone on at her parents' house.

She laughed it off and told me not to worry. 'You just run along and give our love to Jill and Kirsteen.'

By the time I got to the hospital, Gilbert was sitting there with Jill, looking at Kirsteen. Only two people were allowed in with her at one time so Jill offered to step outside as she'd been there all day. 'I'll give you two a chance,' she said ruefully.

'Oh, Kirsteen's beautiful,' Gilbert told me. 'I wish I could give her a squeeze.'

'You'll be able to soon enough,' I said. 'But it takes a bit of getting used to having that plaster against your tummy. It's harder than it looks.'

I could tell as soon as I arrived that Gilbert had already tipped Jill off about my altercation with his wife; Jill was fuming at her mother's selfishness, as I would have expected. But I would have been devastated if I'd thought that I'd caused my father-in-law any offence. Fortunately, as soon as we were alone with Kirsteen, he was quick to put me straight.

'I don't want you worrying about earlier,' he told me.

'I hope I didn't say anything out of turn,' I said.

'Nonsense,' he laughed. 'You deserve a medal for being so restrained.'

It meant a lot to me to hear his reassurances, and he added that he would handle any fallout when he got home.

Like us, Gilbert was keen to learn what had caused Kirsteen's condition. I told him all I knew, which, I realised as I spoke, wasn't a great deal. 'All we really know for sure,' I said, 'is that it was nobody's fault.'

Gilbert sighed. 'But you try telling Jill that?' he guessed.

'Spot on,' I said.

Although I initially had some misgivings, I now absolutely, resolutely believe that it was nobody's fault. We were assured by medical opinion that none of Jill's activities during pregnancy was to blame. There are enough problems in life without trying to apportion blame. Kirsteen's condition is a horrible, unfortunate circumstance that was visited upon us – something over which nobody had any control. I harbour no guilt for myself or for Jill. It just happened.

I stayed with Kirsteen and her grandfather for another half-hour then disappeared into the canteen to allow Jill some more time with her father.

That afternoon brought our first landmark – Jill was allowed to change one of Kirsteen's nappies. She took more time over it than the nurses did, but she desperately wanted to get it right. Kirsteen cried all the way through the whole procedure, and I don't blame her at all. Although, when I think back, our other children were just as put out by their first nappy changes!

I was sure I could have heard Kirsteen's cries from a mile away, and I really felt for her. But one of the nurses assured me that all the noise was perfectly normal. 'It just seems louder to you because you're her father,' she told me.

I watched in awe as Jill was shown how to apply a moist gauze strip to Kirsteen's tummy. We were told that on no account should that area be allowed to dry out. She was too delicate to take risks.

Believe it or not, I couldn't wait to do my first nappy. It can often be a horrible job. But when it's the only chance you get to hold your little girl, you take it with open arms.

That night, I was asked to leave with the normal visitors and Jill was despatched back to the Queen Mother's at the same time. As I said goodbye to her, I was struck by just how exhausted I felt. Adrenaline had carried me through the previous day, and today, there had been the excitement at seeing Kirsteen and the knowledge that I had various logistical needs to fulfil for the boys. But now, knowing I was finally able to go home and relax, tiredness hit me like a ton of bricks.

Before I left I wanted to make sure Jill would rest as well.

'Get along with you,' she told me. 'I'm all right here.'

We assured each other, for our mutual benefit I guess, that tomorrow was another day and that Kirsteen would be noticeably better.

'I couldn't bear it if we had to look at her like this for too long,' Jill said.

I nodded. It didn't bear thinking about.

That night I stayed at home in Milngavie. It seemed eerily quiet without the boys around. I cooked myself a simple meal, then went to bed, and was asleep before my head even hit the pillow.

Early the next morning, I was awoken by the telephone.

Panicking, I grabbed the receiver. If it was bad news about Kirsteen – or Jill – I needed to know.

'Hello?' I said tentatively, desperately trying to shake the sleep from my voice.

My heart lifted only slightly when I heard Gilbert's voice on the other end. What news could he have? Perhaps the hospital hadn't been able to get hold of me so they'd spoken to him?

'Is it Kirsteen?' I asked quickly. 'Or Jill? Is something wrong with one of them?'

'Calm down,' my father-in-law said. 'Nothing's wrong with either of them.'

'Thank God for that,' I said. 'I thought you were ringing with bad news.'

'Ah well,' Gilbert said, 'it depends on how you look at it.'

I was confused. What on earth could he be talking about?

'I was just phoning to tell you,' he continued, 'that my wife is currently standing on Erskine Bridge. She's threatening to throw herself off – and she's blaming you!'

CHAPTER 4

What's the Point in Keeping Them Alive?

KIRSTEEN: I couldn't live without my family. My mum, my dad, my brothers – they're the most important people in my life. Lots of my friends have very close extended families. They've got wonderful grandparents and brilliant aunts and uncles. My dad's parents are great, but live quite far away.

Mum and Dad say it's always been 'us against the world'. For my brothers and me, that's the way it's always been. We don't know any different. But I know that Mum and Dad have been upset over the years by some of their family. They've never told me directly, but I think I was the cause of a lot of arguments. I wish it had been different, for Mum and Dad's sakes. It must be terrible not getting on with your family. I'm lucky. They've always been there for me.

MARTIN: Whenever I tell people I work in the police force and they know where I come from, I always hear the same thing: 'Say hello to Taggart for me.' The television show, which starred Mark McManus, is set just down the road from us at Maryhill Police Office. Like a lot of TV dramas, I don't think it was strictly accurate. If you're a detective inspector working from the Maryhill Police Office you would only be covering Maryhill and Milngavie and not much else besides – hardly a large area when you consider all the crimes that took place in the programme. Yet, in practice Taggart and his successors seemed to have a much more roving franchise. Their patch spread all over Glasgow and beyond.

But for a young cop it's fun to see your local territory portrayed on a successful television series. It's not like watching Hill Street Blues where the action takes place so far away – with Taggart you could actually think, 'I know those streets. I've arrested people there.' Or even, 'He shouldn't have gone that way – there's a short cut if he'd have taken the next road.'

Taggart isn't the reason I joined the force though. I've lived in Milngavie more or less all my life, although my family are actually English. My parents are both what the Scottish would call 'southerners' – my dad's from St Helens and my mum's from Prescot, both in Merseyside. But Dad got a job with BICC Cables in the 1950s and was transferred to Glasgow, and so I was born here.

I was educated at Milngavie Primary School and then Douglas Academy and, I have to admit, I was nothing special – pretty middle-of-the-road all the way. The one subject I really felt I could get my teeth into was photography, although finding work as a photographer is easier said than done. After a lot of anguish and soul-searching I realised there was no future for me in straightforward photography and decided to be a bit more creative with my career plans. I discovered there was a way in which I could use my photography skills in another industry, although it might take a few years to get there. That's how I ended up in Strathclyde Police where, at the time of writing, I've been for twenty-six years.

I joined the police force on 15 February 1982 and spent ten years on uniform duty in the communities of Clydebank and Drumchapel. I was never interested in winning promotions for the sake of career progress, so when I eventually sat my sergeant's exam, it wasn't because I wanted more responsibility or to look better. My goal was to get into a department called the Identification Bureau where I would be able to use the photographic skills I had acquired through study and practice in my spare time all those years earlier.

I'm generally a laid-back sort of character, but being told I'd been accepted in 1991 really meant a lot to me. As much as I'd enjoyed the day-to-day relationships in my community police work, this was where my heart was. Working with a camera was my dream when I left school and now I was living that dream – although perhaps not in the fashion that my Douglas Academy tutors might have expected.

My Identification Bureau duties were principally photographing crime scenes and collecting evidence, initially by gathering fingerprints. You've probably seen people doing my job in any number of Hollywood movies. We're the ones that crawl under the yellow police tape while the uniformed officers hold the press back. It could be a housebreaking, as we say in Scotland, or even a murder – whenever it was felt there might be evidence to be found, we would be summoned. Typically, attending officers would seal the place in question, then call in senior officers, CID investigating officers, who would come along and assess from outside. Next, we would be called in to capture the evidence in photographs and video before anyone had the chance to contaminate the scene. It was important work. Everything had to be properly recorded. The pictures we took would need to stand up in court. The work we did on any given day would need to survive long after police officers' memories had become a little hazy with the passage of time.

There were many of us in the department, about sixty in all, but we all always seemed to be busy. I attended a lot of very high-profile crime scenes, working all hours, attending call-outs any time of the day or night.

Despite the occasional gruesome nature of the work I went on to spend thirteen very happy years in the evidence-gathering section of the Identification Bureau – or Scene Examination Branch as it became known – until in 2004, as DNA testing and other more accurate techniques emerged, reliance on departments like ours increased dramatically to the point where we struggled to cope. For political reasons, it was considered more economical to use civilian staff in the department rather than police officers.

From a personal point of view, I was sad to see it come to an end. After so long working at the sharp end of the criminal system it felt like a demotion to be put back into uniform duties in the city-centre division. Although my new role still involves fingerprinting and forensic work, I admit I found the transition quite hard.

Another change to affect me, though, is the recent decision to move the local divisional boundaries. Bizarrely, my area of remit has been altered to encompass Drum-chapel. So after twenty-six years I'm covering the same area as when I started.

I thought of my job that morning as I took the call from my father-in-law, Gilbert. He seemed so matter-of-fact and unimpressed about Gay's threat to jump off the Erskine Bridge that I found it difficult to take it seriously myself. I knew she had some history of this sort of behaviour, but I also knew that at some point down the line the police would have to be called. It's such a tight community, I wondered if I would receive any flak. If my mother-in-law had anything to do with it, I was sure I would.

'I'm so sorry, Gilbert,' I told him. I was genuinely sad to have put him through this. 'Is there anything I can do?'

'No,' he said. 'I've already driven up to her and asked her to get in the car but she told me to clear off.' He chuckled. 'So now I'm watching her through binoculars. She'll never do it. But I wonder how long she'll stay out there.'

I told Gilbert to keep me posted. Later that day he filled me in on what had happened. After our row Gay had gone into some sort of a fury, then she'd marched off to the bridge and said she wasn't coming back.

'Half an hour after I tried to collect her,' Gilbert said, 'the bridge patrol picked her up and brought her home. They obviously ticked her off a bit and then a while after that the police arrived.'

'I bet it all came out that it was my fault,' I said.

'Oh it did that, all right,' Gilbert laughed. 'She wanted them to charge you with all sorts. The officers said they knew you.'

I was concerned that my career could be affected but Gilbert assured me that I had no need to worry. 'From what

I could tell, they were more angry with her than with anyone else. She didn't understand that she was wasting police time. But why would she?' He sighed.

I fretted about that episode for a while. It only needs one person in your workplace to take against you and then something like this gets blown out of all proportion. But as it turned out, Gilbert was right. I never heard from those policemen, or even discovered who they were.

I lost an awful lot of respect for my mother-in-law that night. But at least she wasn't my mother. Jill had had to put up with her all her life.

JILL: I didn't see my mother for seven months after Kirsteen was born. She blamed it on her falling out with Martin. They'd had that silly argument about my nephew John's exams. But that wasn't the reason she never visited me in hospital.

The reason was Kirsteen. She didn't want to see her.

And I knew why.

I spent a lot of my first night in hospital crying with worry about Kirsteen and what had happened to her in that operating theatre. And of course I was petrified that I'd caused it somehow. 'What if I'd eaten the wrong sort of cheese?' There's that whole list of dos and don'ts for mums-to-be. I'd always followed it to the letter. But what if I'd made a mistake?

On the second night, once I'd seen Kirsteen in that ward in Yorkhill, plugged into all those machines, I was happy that she was going to be all right. The doctors had told us there was nothing to worry about, and I knew that from a medical point of view they were right. Martin and I would give her the best standard of care that we could and she'd want for nothing from us. If there was a medical avenue to explore we'd be down it with torches and maps.

But I also knew that the rest of my family didn't think like that.

As I was lying in the Queen Mother's on that second night, confident that Kirsteen was out of the woods, I knew that from my mother's perspective I'd brought shame on my family.

I remembered that when I was five years old we'd been told by her not to play with a girl in the village who had polio. She was afraid for us to be around anything that was not perfect. If she ever heard about a poor baby who'd been born with Down's syndrome or some other ailment, she'd say, 'They should have been dropped on their head when they were born. What's the point in keeping them alive? They are just a drain on society.'

Looking back, I'm amazed I was able to distance myself from her views. It's so easy to go along with whatever your parents tell you. But I always knew there was something wrong with her train of thought. After all, my father was a dentist and spent his whole life trying to help people, and with a child's simplicity I thought, 'They can't all be bad just because they need fillings in their mouths?'

I know there are still many people in this world who look on things in the way my mother did, and I don't know how they live with themselves. Disabled people can bring as much joy to the world as anyone else. Nobody is perfect, and just because you may look it from the outside doesn't mean you are that way on the inside.

I was terrified about what my mother would say when she found out Kirsteen was disabled. But it never occurred to me that she would simply ignore me. Seven months is a long time in a child's life. She missed all of Kirsteen's big moments and I'll never forgive that.

But that's the way I was brought up and I knew, more or less, what to expect. I had rejected my mother's values, and I know my sister Suzanne had as well, but I wasn't as close to my brother Sam, or to my eldest sister Gladys. I didn't know what they would think.

One thing I did know was that my world would fall apart if my father shared my mother's thoughts. I needn't have worried though. My father was a great man when I was growing up and he was a great man until the day he died. He and Suzanne were the only members of my family who really spoke to me in those early days. You can't imagine how lonely I felt. But seeing my father made all the difference.

My father was a wonderful man who could not do enough for anybody. Nobody had a bad word to say against him. I wondered why Dad stuck with his marriage, but he always did. I guess he thought it was the right thing to do. And my dad always did the right thing.

My grandfather had been a dentist and my father and uncle followed in his footsteps. They could have just enjoyed the city life but they knew there were others out there who needed their help, so they took their practice around the islands. They bought a 65-foot boat and had it converted into a surgery, then one week out of every month they'd leave their practice in Glasgow and head out to the tiny wee islands. They went up to Muck and Eigg. They even took their practice to places as out of the way as Tobermory, Tiree and Colonsay.

I'm sure it wouldn't comply with health and safety regulations these days, but that boat had everything needed to run a surgery. All the equipment, the drugs, electricity and running water. They even administered general anaesthetics on it. Where else were those islanders going to get treatment? Hundreds of people depended on my father and uncle making their journeys. And they loved it as well. It was an adventure for them. I don't think they earned much money from it, but they made people healthy and themselves happy. Two out of three isn't bad.

That was my father all over. Always wanting to give something back. When he was working on dry land I think he must have made quite a bit of money. The four of us – with just five years between us – were sent to a fee-paying school in Glasgow, about ten miles away from home. We had a part-time gardener, a cleaner, new Jaguar cars every couple of years and decent holidays. It sounds idyllic. But there was a problem.

My mother had wanted four boys. She got three girls and one boy. She told us all from a young age that she was disappointed with the hand she'd been dealt. Suzanne, a year older than me, and I were openly disliked by our mother. She didn't mind the oldest daughter and loved her son, obviously. I sometimes come across people who say they sensed something similar in their own families. Well, I didn't have to sense it. My mother told me outright. To my face.

I adored my father. I would have done anything for him and it was no surprise to anyone when I announced that I wanted to follow his professional example and become a dental nurse. I started out in his practice, which was interesting but hard work. Then I got involved with community dentistry and worked around all the islands. Not in the boat, thank goodness, but it was still quite a journey.

I'd go round the various communities giving talks in places like Tobermory, Iona, Lochgilphead and Oban. It was a good life for a single girl and I continued with it until I had children.

My dad was such a great role model that my brother became a dentist as well. He actually took it a stage further and became a professor of dentistry at Dundee.

As children we were encouraged to play golf – another sign of our comfortable lifestyle, golf never having been a poor man's sport. Suzanne and Gladys threw themselves into it and they both represented Scotland in the Curtis Cup. Suzanne was actually the world junior golf champion, winning every title there was to win as an amateur. But I was never interested. It was politics that caught my attention when I was young, and that was what took up all my spare time.

If it hadn't, I would never have met Martin.

MARTIN: I blame Helen Swann.

I met Jill on the day of the general election in 1987. I was on duty at the polling station in Barclay Church in Old Kirkpatrick and she was an election agent for the Tory Party. We were a captive audience for each other for sixteen hours that day. And everything else just went from there. But it very nearly didn't happen. It wouldn't have happened at all, in fact, if it weren't for a colleague of mine called Helen Swann.

From a policing point of view, working at a polling station involves nothing more than physically being there. Our job is just to be a presence, to ensure that there is no disorder, either inside or outside. It's the same every general election. Compulsory overtime shift across the board, giving us a long, long day to kill.

I had actually been pencilled in to cover a polling station at Drumchapel. Helen Swann was down for Old Kirkpatrick. The day before, however, her car broke down and so she asked to be posted somewhere closer to home.

'I don't see why not,' the sergeant told her. 'Leave it with me.'

He then put it to me, and as I was living in a flat in Old Kirkpatrick at the time it suited me fine. Every time I see Helen now I say, 'It's all your fault.' She takes it in good part, but really, if it weren't for the unreliability of her Mini, there wouldn't be a story to tell.

What also worked in our favour that day was Jill's temper. She had been scheduled to juggle her time outside this polling station plus another one up the road. Unfortunately, or fortunately as it turned out, she got into an argument with an election agent for the Labour Party there and was banned from the premises. That gave her plenty of time to kill with me. I can't remember what we spoke about, but I recall feeling more and more agitated the longer the day went on. I realised I was falling for this fiery young politico and found myself thinking: 'If I haven't asked her out before this shift ends I'm mad.'

I did and we started seeing each other after that. Two and a half years later we were married.

Right from the start I could tell that Jill's family were a little bit out of the ordinary. Her brother Sam was on a totally different intellectual plane and was so serious I always found it very hard to make any headway with him. There was no common interest between us and it was almost impossible to have a laugh with him.

Jill's eldest sister, Gladys, was always the special one. At least as far as Gay was concerned. She showed obvious and bizarre favouritism towards her throughout her kids' child-hoods.

After Kirsteen was born and Gay made it known that she wasn't talking to me and that she wouldn't be seeing her new granddaughter either, I guessed that it must have been awkward for Gilbert to keep visiting.

'I appreciate you coming along every day,' I told him.

'I wouldn't miss seeing my granddaughter for the world,' he said.

'I hope you're not getting any criticism for it at home.'

He shrugged – a gesture that told me everything I needed to know. But he still came back the next day. And the next.

A true gentleman.

Even so, Jill and I were soon to discover that once we left the security of the hospital walls, we were on our own. The question neither of us dared to ask was: could we cope?

CHAPTER 5

I Don't Belong Here

KIRSTEEN: As I got older I learned that hospitals are frightening places for everyone – not just the person undergoing treatment. It's natural for all eyes to be focused on the patient in the bed. But they're the ones in the best hands. Dozens of nurses and doctors are looking out for their every need and millions of pounds' worth of equipment is at their disposal should it be required.

In lots of hospitals, however, there's often very little in the way of support for the families of patients. They seem to get forgotten in the whirlwind of activity. It's only as I reached my teens that I realised how hard it must have been for my parents to come and sit with me every day. I didn't understand that they'd had to put their lives on hold to spend time with me. Dad had his job, Mum had my brothers to think about. What they really needed was a bit more help from their families. But I don't think they got that. And as soon as I was old enough to appreciate that, I felt more guilty than ever.

MARTIN: When Kirsteen was born I wanted to spend as much time at Yorkhill as I could but I also had to make provision for the boys. Gilbert, bless him, did as much as he could – but he himself was in and out of hospital over the years with asthma, angina and artery problems, so we could only lean on him so much. Suzanne helped out as well. But the real gap in my life was my own parents.

I've never had any fallings-out with them, in the way that Jill has had with her family so regularly, but there is considerable geographical distance between us.

My mum never really settled in Milngavie. She didn't have many friends in Scotland at all, and strayed very little outside her own comfort zone. She would walk into Milngavie town centre, about fifteen minutes away, do a bit of shopping, then come home and just get on with running the house. She did that every single day, apart from Sundays, I think out of habit rather than enjoyment. Every chance we got, and whenever my dad's work allowed, we would visit Mum's relatives down in Prescot. I loved going there because there were so many aunts and uncles and cousins to meet. But afterwards we would drive back across the border and Mum would slot back into her routine. She never complained about it, nor did she appear to be unhappy. But she didn't seem particularly happy either.

My father took early retirement when he was sixty and, as if an opportunity had suddenly presented itself to my mother, they packed their bags shortly after, in 1985, and moved back to Merseyside. I was still living at home at the time so that was when I moved into my flat in Old Kirkpatrick. I lived there for four years, during which time I met Jill. It makes me sad to think that for all the time Jill and I have been together, my parents have lived hundreds of miles away. And it's at times of great stress, when you're visiting two people in hospital, while at the same time trying to keep two young boys happy, that you realise just how isolated you have become.

My parents came up just after Kirsteen's birth, which was a great help. They looked after the boys while I was at the hospital, and when they went in to see Kirsteen and Jill, that gave me the chance to spend some time at home with Kenneth and Martin, as though everything was normal. With all that was going on at Yorkhill, it was important they didn't feel left out.

Having my parents around for those few days lifted a lot of the pressure off me. They also came up again once we were allowed to take Kirsteen home.

My parents are now in their eighties, and their age and distance have conspired so that our relationship is pretty much based on a five-minute phone call on a Sunday and, perhaps, seeing each other for a couple of days each year. They've helped us out financially a few times, for which we've been very grateful, but circumstances mean that they are no longer able to provide any physical help.

Apart from the early visits after Kirsteen was born, we had no one to take the day-to-day strain off us in the way that other young couples might have if their family was on the doorstep.

Gilbert did his best, but soon after Kirsteen came along he became quite infirm. And now, with Kirsteen's condition likely to cause unknown problems in the future, I knew my parents wouldn't often be there to help with her either.

As I made the lonely drive to visit Kirsteen and Jill on the third day, I really wished they could.

JILL: Martin's parents are lovely people and I really like them, but his dad was seventy when Kirsteen was born and was already starting to feel he was too old to be shuttling up and down motorways. I also think that because Martin's sister had children much earlier than we did, they'd already had their grandchildren, seen them grow up and enjoyed them. It was as if they felt too old to be going through it all again now.

All the other little boys and girls in Yorkhill had lots of people visiting them – parents, brothers, sisters, aunts, uncles and grandparents – and, as I looked at Kirsteen, I felt that we were selling her short by not having more relatives cooing over her. She was too young to notice, of course, but one day she would.

Still, I do wish we'd been able to see more of my in-laws. For our own sakes and the kids'.

When Martin arrived to see me on the third day, these were just some of the things that were rushing around my mind. I wished I could have stopped them but it was virtually impossible. Nights spent on your own in hospital are terrible experiences. You're trapped in your bed, with only your thoughts for company. And they're never good thoughts. All your darkest fears and worries surface when the lights go out and you're left with the sounds of the other patients sleeping or reading, and the bustle of nurses around you. It's so difficult having your nearest and dearest sent away from you. When you're ill is when you need people the most. It seems barbaric that that's when you're separated from them. So I couldn't wait to see

Martin and share my fears with him, but he had his own worries.

'The boys are really missing you, Jill,' he said. 'And they can't wait to see their little sister.'

'I'm not sure they're ready to see her with all the tubes in,' I said. 'But I won't be in here for long now.'

'Let's not be hasty,' Martin said. 'The doctors explained that you'll have to rest in here a fair while yet.'

I think they let women out earlier these days, but back then a week seemed to be the minimum stay after a Caesarean. I wasn't convinced I would be there that long, though. All I could think of was my little girl in the other building. The sooner I was discharged, the sooner I felt I could really get down to looking after her seriously. My stitches would have to worry about themselves.

Martin understood how I felt. It was hard for him – concerned as he was about me in one hospital and Kirsteen in another. But I would have swapped places with him in a heartbeat. He couldn't possibly know what I was going through in that hospital bed. He couldn't have a clue how painful it was for me there.

MARTIN: Jill fell pregnant with Kenneth almost as soon as we got married. We'd been a couple for two and a half years by then and we had about nine months as newlyweds before Kenneth came along. We've devoted ourselves to being parents for virtually our entire marriage, and I'll admit that at times I've felt like a wrung-out rag – always jumping between work, home or hospital. I can't complain though. Any father would do it, and I'm sure there are plenty of people who have a harder time than I do.

I remember finding out she was pregnant that first time.

'Bloody hell! I knew it was going to happen one day but this is a bit soon,' I said.

Jill was as surprised as I was. Having children was definitely part of our plan, but timing-wise it caught us unawares. We were both delighted though because Jill was coming up to thirty, which was considered quite old, at that time, to be having your first.

After the initial excitement had passed, I began to worry about practicalities. At the time I was working in the three-shift system at Drumchapel and Jill was a dental nurse with the Argyle and Clyde community health board, so we were both bringing in a full-time wage. But we soon decided that Jill wouldn't be going back to work after the baby came, even though we knew it would mean tough times to come. It was important for us to do as much for our new family as possible. If there were nappies to be changed or feeds to be given, we wanted to be the ones doing it. What sense was there in paying a nursery or someone else to do it for us?

We were living in a little terraced house then, just around the corner from where we live now. A recession was forecast, interest rates were soaring and, at one stage, we were struggling to keep up with our 15 per cent mortgage rate repayments. Financial hardship threatened to temper our joy to some extent, but we were expecting our first baby and that was all that mattered.

Like a lot of men, I concentrated most of my thoughts on the issues of money and how we were all going to live. Jill thought about the baby every minute of the day, whereas I mainly thought about it when I saw her in the mornings and evenings. In between I had work to do. And then there was all the shopping – kitting our house out with cots and clothes, and getting the baby's room ready.

When Jill went into labour at the end of September 1990, it was one of the happiest and also most anxious days of my life; I'm sure all first-time parents go through this. When it became apparent that there were complications with the birth, I thought my worst fears were about to be realised, but from the moment Jill was rushed through for an emergency Caesarean everything happened so quickly, and so painlessly, that I didn't even have time to be scared. By a strange coincidence, our second baby was born in the same manner at the end of April 1992. But it wasn't such a shock the second time round. Each baby is special but you never forget the first time you go through these things.

JILL: I was ecstatic when I finally went into labour. We tried to deliver Kenneth without surgery, so I felt I'd tried to do the 'right' thing. But lying in the operating theatre, I knew the most important thing was getting him out safe and sound. It didn't matter that it was a Caesarean section.

When I finally set eyes on him for the first time, I burst out crying. I kept thinking, he's mine, my first child. You don't really know what to expect, then, suddenly, you're overwhelmed by emotions. You feel such love, such responsibility. I couldn't believe we'd done it.

Martin was crying too. He was as delighted as I was. During the pregnancy I'd been thinking about the baby all the time and getting worked up about it, but Martin just took it all in his stride.

But when Kenneth was born he was all over him. He couldn't wait to get him home, to take him for walks. He just wanted to be with him all the time. I think it was real for him suddenly. He was very hands-on, right from the start, wanting to spend as much time with Kenneth as possible. He was in the hospital every second that he was allowed, desperate to be with his wife and child.

It was the same when Martin came along. And it was the same now with Kirsteen.

But this time his baby was kept in a different place from me.

Whatever pain Martin was going through, I was suffering as well. We were in the same terrible position. But it was after he went home and before he arrived that my nightmares began.

It started on the first night. I was in a ward with seven other women. Next to their beds were the little perspex boxes that held their babies. I was shattered when I got back from Yorkhill the first night after spending time with the doctors and seeing Kirsteen after her operation.

I fell asleep as soon as my head hit the pillow. I felt as though I hadn't closed my eyes for days. But my rest was short-lived. About two hours later – although it felt like just seconds – I was awake. A baby was screaming. I could hear its tired mother struggling to comfort it, getting stressed because the baby wouldn't feed. Then she started crying as well. I knew what that exhausted desperation felt like. She was going through hell, but all I could think was: I wish that was me. I would have given anything to have had my little girl next to me, with getting her to feed the only thing I had to worry about.

I think I was woken up at least six more times that night by the other babies. But worse was to come before Martin arrived the next day.

A lot of people work in hospitals and faces come and go. Every time there's a shift change, you see someone else.

There are three shifts in a day, one every eight hours. That means you can see half a dozen nurses a day, sometimes more. They're all trained to make new mums and their babies as comfortable as possible. But they're not mind-readers, and they assume that you're the same as everyone else on the ward.

That first morning was the worst. It was a nurse I hadn't seen before and she hadn't been told about Kirsteen.

'Hello, Mrs Lupton, how are you feeling today?' she said cheerily from the foot of my bed. 'Where's your wee baby?' Without waiting for an answer she unhooked the clipboard to read my notes.

I couldn't help it. I broke down.

It was torture. I couldn't begrudge those other mums their happiness. But why did I have to share a room with them? I was in a maternity ward, but I didn't have a baby with me, and that broke my heart.

'I don't belong here,' I'd told Martin.

'But it's the best place for you,' he'd said. 'You're a patient too.'

And I knew he was right. But still I'd wondered why I had to be surrounded by all those smiling young mums with their healthy, noisy, crying, beautiful babies.

And after three nights of the same hell I made a decision.

'I'm signing myself out,' I told the head nurse on duty that morning. 'I want to leave.'

She looked shocked. 'Mrs Lupton, you're still not recovered. It's bad enough you gallivanting to and fro along to Yorkhill. You're not giving your body a chance to recover. I'll have to ask the doctor.'

'Don't ask him – tell him,' I said. 'I'm going home. I can't take it here any longer.'

Martin was just as shocked when he arrived a few hours later.

'I've made up my mind,' I told him. 'Don't try to stop me. You've no idea what it's like in here. It's torture.'

He knew there was no point in arguing with me. If only those doctors and nurses had been as sensible. But they were only doing their jobs, I suppose.

MARTIN: It felt weird on that fourth day, knowing that Jill would be coming home with me later.

We were both at Kirsteen's bedside while Jill's sister looked after the boys. We were allowed to change her nappy again, and by now she'd been taken off the drip, so we could feed her as well. It was wonderful to watch Jill hold a bottle to our daughter's little mouth and to see her taking her first sips. After everything Kirsteen had been through, I had half expected this to become another problem, but there were no hitches. It took a bit of practice but soon she was gulping away.

Every time I looked at her I was saddened by the plaster. I wondered when she cried whether it may have been because she had an itch. How would she be able to tell us? It was hard enough knowing when she was sleepy or hungry. How would she let us know that her knee needed scratching?

At lunchtime I went to take the boys off Suzanne's hands, and left Gilbert with Jill. When I returned to collect her at six, it was with two little boys in tow. They hadn't seen their mother for four days. They'd never been separated for so long – and it showed. There were tears all round as I loaded the luggage into the car.

'Mummy's coming home,' Jill told Kenneth. 'And she's never going to leave you again.' Martin was clinging on to her neck like his life depended on it. I hoped they didn't think she'd left them by choice.

Both boys were asleep by the time we got home. They didn't know it, but the next day they would be seeing their sister for the first time.

CHAPTER 6

We're Going Home

KIRSTEEN: Being the youngest in my family, I can't imagine what it must be like having a little brother or sister. Martin was too young to appreciate what was going on, I think, but Kenneth understood that he was being taken to see me for the first time. Mum and Dad told him that I was in a special place where doctors and nurses were looking after me. I think they were worried that he'd be upset when he saw me. But to a three-year-old everything in a hospital looks out of the ordinary. He probably didn't think it odd at all that I was in plaster from the waist down.

MARTIN: For the next few days our life settled into something of a routine. Each day Jill would go into Yorkhill and sit with Kirsteen and help out as much as possible. We were allowed to hold and cuddle her – the plaster made her a little heavier than you'd expect for a baby of her size, but it meant so much to us to pick her up and tell her we loved her. We'd been told that she would be in the neonatal surgery ward for four or five weeks, so there was nothing for it but to hunker down and get our lives into as much a semblance of normality as we could manage.

While Jill went in every day in that first week, I stayed with the boys. It was actually a refreshing change for me to have them all to myself – usually Jill was the main carer and I did my bit before work, when I got home in the evenings or at weekends. It was nice to have what I would call quality time with them, but I couldn't forget what had given me that chance. I had two weeks' paternity leave and should have been spending it with Kirsteen.

Each day I went in to Yorkhill and took the boys with me. The first time Kenneth saw his little sister you could see he was confused, but that didn't stop him wanting a big cuddle with her. For Martin, who was just beginning to walk at the time, there were plenty of interesting things in the ward that caught his eye. It was quite exhausting keeping tabs on the boys' whereabouts. But it was worth it for what it meant to us. For an hour or so every day we had the whole family in the same room. All five of us Luptons together.

It was a difficult time, but at least we had some consistency back in our lives – Jill being back at home made all the difference. It was of paramount importance to us that the boys didn't feel they were second best to Kirsteen. They were too young to understand that she was ill, and we didn't want them thinking we were choosing to spend time with her over them. They needed to feel that they were getting equal treatment; that meant not passing them from pillar to post, which is why I opted to spend time at home with them rather than be with Jill every day at the hospital. But at least one of us was with Kirsteen at all times.

As much of a relief as it was to me to have Jill back home, I had to occasionally remind myself that she was not 100 per cent fit either. I know the doctors hadn't wanted her to leave the Queen Mother's when she did; in fact, they'd asked me to try to persuade her to stay, explaining that if she continued to do as she was, there would be a serious risk of her wound opening up. I discussed it with Jill, but the most important thing in the world to her was getting out. And that's Jill all over. She'll do anything a doctor suggests for one of her children, but places her own health very much down the list of priorities. And you really can't stop her once she's made her mind up.

As hard as all the toing and froing was in that first week or so, I knew it was going to get much worse, and the idea of going back to work while the boys still needed looking after was actually quite worrying.

Before my leave was over I called my senior officer and explained the situation. He was very good about it. He said that they couldn't give me time off, not paid – and we needed every penny at this stage – but he'd be happy for my lunch hours to be spent at the hospital. Fortunately, because of the work I did, I was quite mobile. Our police van covered the Strathclyde area, so it was fairly straightforward for me to be dropped off at Yorkhill each day, then picked up an hour so later. But that wasn't really the issue at that stage; it was taking care of the boys that was the problem.

Often Gilbert would keep them entertained for a couple of hours at the hospital while Jill stayed at Kirsteen's bedside. Generally, the boys were on their best behaviour at the hospital while Jill and I talked (my visits were our only opportunity to catch up – for me on the latest from the doctors, for her on the comings and goings in the outside world), but short of strapping them in their prams, you can't keep a three- and one-and-a-half-year-old completely still.

The nurses were always very good about working around them and would stop to have a chat with them whenever they could. But one day, Kirsteen had a visit from Mr Fyfe, and as we were talking to him I became aware of the noise from the boys getting louder. I think they were a little fractious because they'd been at the hospital for a few hours by that point. Suddenly there was a crash and Kenneth's juice was all over the floor and down his clothes. In no time at all, one of the nurses had wiped Kenneth down, while another mopped the floor, and I thought nothing further of it. It was just 'one of those things' that any parent gets used to.

It was only later that I learned there would be repercussions.

I kissed Kirsteen and Jill goodbye and took the boys out with me. I just had time to drop them off at their aunt's before starting my next shift. In four hours' time I'd collect them again and we'd all go back over to Yorkhill.

As we arrived at the neonatal surgery ward that evening, a nurse came over to me. I recognised her as one of Kirsteen's regular carers, and greeted her cheerily. But something in her manner was different. Was it my imagination or was she not altogether pleased to see us?

'I'm sorry, Mr Lupton,' she began, 'but I'm afraid your wee boys won't be allowed into the ward any more.'

I couldn't believe what I was hearing.

'You're welcome to take them into the waiting room, but I'm afraid the ward is off limits from now on.'

I was ready to leap to my boys' defence, but I was more confused than angry. 'I don't understand,' I said. 'They've always been allowed in before.'

The nurse didn't reply.

'Has there been a complaint?' I asked.

'I'm sorry, Mr Lupton,' she said and we both knew what she wasn't able to say. Mr Fyfe had not looked too pleased that afternoon. He had given the order to ban the boys from his ward.

I was directed to a little anteroom at the end of the ward – a day room, where more mobile patients could read or watch television. I set the boys down there, then ran to the ward and beckoned Jill out. I explained what had transpired.

'What's he gone and done that for?' she exploded. 'They're only tiny. I think they behave bloody well cooped up in here all the time.'

I was just as angry as Jill was, but there was no point arguing. Mr Fyfe obviously thought he was doing the best for his patients, but I don't think he appreciated what an impact his decision would have on our lives. At that time, the only way I could see my wife was when we were both sitting with Kirsteen; if the boys were banned from going in, then one of us would have to leave our baby in order to sit with them outside. We'd never see each other.

I already felt like my life had become something of a plate-spinning act, and, with this news, the chances of me dropping as plate had just increased tenfold.

JILL: It was a ridiculous way to carry on. Martin was already running around all over town, trying to do his job, then sort the boys out, then come into the hospital a couple of times a day. Then, when we were told that the boys were no longer allowed on the ward, I wondered what else could go wrong.

I didn't know it then, but help was just around the corner.

Five days after Kirsteen was born a doctor came to the house to check on me. I welcomed him into the lounge and waited for him to begin discussing my operation scars. But he wasn't interested in my physical well-being; it was my mind he was concerned about.

'I know it's been a stressful time for you, Mrs Lupton, and you probably had quite a shock at the birth,' he said. 'I wonder, can you tell me: how do you feel about your daughter now?'

'Well, I'm naturally upset,' I replied. I recalled that when they'd first told us about Kirsteen's condition, I hadn't cried immediately because it hadn't surprised me. Was it possible that someone had reported me to the mental-health unit because of that?

The doctor looked at me and said, 'Would you say you were depressed?'

'I suppose so,' I answered, thinking what an odd question it was.

That was the answer he appeared to be waiting for. He jumped to life and, as he wrote out a prescription for a new drug called Seroxat, he said, 'OK, I want you to take these tablets. They'll help you. And don't worry,' he added, before I could even ask, 'they're non-addictive.'

To be honest with you I couldn't wait to get to the chemist and get the prescription filled. I felt a little chemical boost would be just what I needed to get to grips with my new life as a mother of three. It wasn't that I didn't want to visit Kirsteen each morning, or to look after the boys every other minute of the day. It was just that I was finding the logistics of it all a bit wearing.

What had we done to deserve all this? I kept thinking. So

much seemed to be conspiring against us. I just prayed that the Seroxat would see me through the next few weeks.

While I waited for the prescribed treatment to kick in, life had to continue. Every day Martin would come by with our sons and we'd swap rooms. He'd go in and have an hour with Kirsteen, while I played with the boys in the day room. We were like ships in the night. There was no time to sit down and discuss anything. By the time we got home each night we were both too exhausted to do anything other than fall into bed and get ready for another day on the treadmill.

But Martin and I had important things to talk about. Our doctor was a man who liked to play his cards close to his chest, so we had begun to make enquiries about bladder exstrophy elsewhere. During one of our fleeting conversations Martin said he'd found a support group specifically for people suffering from the condition and their families.

'It's called BEES,' he told me, 'which stands for Bladder Exstrophy and Epispadias Support.' (Epispadias is a condition that affects boys' genitals, whereas bladder exstrophy, although more common in boys, also affects girls.)

We got in touch with BEES as soon as possible; it wasn't going to help Kirsteen get better, or make our day-to-day life any easier, but it made me feel less worried about her, and I found it helpful just knowing that other people out there were experiencing the same sort of feelings as we were. But I wasn't prepared for some of the things I learned.

One of the first people we spoke to from the group told us that she'd had the same premonition about her baby as I'd had about Kirsteen.

'I just knew there was something wrong.'

'Did you have all the scans?' we asked her.

'Four – and an amniocentesis.'

Nobody had believed me when I'd said that something was wrong with my baby and this woman had been through exactly the same thing. And as convinced as I had been that I was right, there was still a tiny part of me that thought I might have been cracking up. Now, however, I knew that I was perfectly sane – and that I was not alone.

But we made another discovery that caused me quite a lot of distress – even though it should have had the opposite effect.

I had a lot of time to myself during the first few weeks of Kirsteen's life and my mind kept coming back to the same few topics. One of them I didn't even dare mention to Martin any more because he got so angry with me: the question of blame. He kept telling me it wasn't anyone's fault and I knew he was right. But I couldn't make it go away. Deep down, I felt there had to be a reason for what had happened to Kirsteen. She was in my body when the condition developed, so it made sense that I must be responsible somehow. And, having bottled these feelings up at home, I couldn't help pouring my heart out, when speaking to some of the other women at BEES.

I wasn't prepared for what they told me.

While there is no definite cause for bladder exstrophy, I learned, there is some evidence to suggest that the male gene could be a significant contributory factor. It's by no means conclusive but the mere fact it was a possibility hadn't even occurred to me – or my husband.

'Are you saying that Martin is more likely to be to blame than I am?' I asked.

'Well, no. No one's to blame exactly, but according to some tests the condition is thought to start with the male side.'

I was so angry as I waited for Martin to come home that night. Not because I wanted to punish him for Kirsteen's condition, but because he'd never once thought it could have been him. I'd been ripping myself apart for weeks, convinced I'd done something wrong. I was certain I must have lifted something, eaten something, got too tired, had too hot a bath. It was the only logical conclusion: something I had done must have caused Kirsteen's condition. Why couldn't it have happened to me and not my daughter? I'd kept asking myself. Why couldn't it be me? But I'd never heard Martin say that.

'How could you let me think it's my fault and never have considered it could be yours?' I screamed the moment he stepped through the door, as three weeks worth of pent-up aggression flooded out of me. 'You didn't even think it could have been you that caused it!'

I told him what I'd discovered that day, and it's fair to say he was shell-shocked.

'I always said you shouldn't blame yourself; it's no one's fault,' he tried to comfort me.

'But I couldn't help blaming myself. It's only natural. But you never thought it might have been something to do with you.'

It was a spectacular argument. My mother would have been proud. I knew it wouldn't turn the clocks back, and I also knew it wasn't Martin's fault that Kirsteen had been born the way she was. But I had to let him know I'd been suffering feelings of guilt since the moment she was born – so why hadn't he?

MARTIN: That was a low point. Feelings had been running high since Kirsteen was born, and I think we'd both bottled up a lot of emotion. Just trying to juggle the day-to-day practicalities with trying to ensure the best care for Kirsteen meant there weren't too many occasions for real heart-to-hearts. But that argument came as a blow. Jill likes to rant and rave, and I can take a lot of it with a bucket of salt, but some of it can be quite hurtful and does have a lasting effect.

That evening she was screaming at me, telling me that men are responsible for bladder exstrophy so if it's anyone's fault, it must be mine. She was furious that I hadn't taken responsibility early on when she was blaming herself. But I couldn't do it. Had the doctors told me it was something to do with me then maybe that would have been different. But they'd assured us it was 'one of those things'.

Kirsteen's condition is a horrible, unfortunate circumstance that neither Jill nor I had any control over. We ate the right things, drank the right things and did the right things – just as we did with the boys. If I'm genetically to blame, so be it. But I can't harbour any guilt for myself or for Jill. We have to get on with our lives. We have to get on with making Kirsteen's life as pain-free as we possibly can.

I think eventually I got my message over to Jill. There was a lot of soul-searching that night, and for a few nights after. It's hard to talk when you're rarely in the same room. But we knew we had to move forwards as a united front for Kirsteen's sake.

And the best way we could do this was to prepare for her coming home.

I remember when Mr Fyfe broke the news.

'You mean she can leave?' I asked.

He nodded. 'The plaster's coming off in the morning. We'll run some tests and she'll require some physio, but all being well, she'll be free to go the day after.'

It was the news we had wanted to hear. It was the news that, as a family, we needed to hear.

But it was also tinged with regret.

When the day came, we should have been ecstatic to take our little girl home. Jill summed up the mood perfectly. 'So many other babies who are born with things wrong have surgical procedures, get fixed up, cured and sent home.'

'But we're going home now,' I reassured her.

'Only until the next time.'

And it was true. We already had an appointment for Kirsteen's next operation. And even that wasn't promised as the final one. 'One step at a time,' Mr Fyfe had told us, and we just prayed he knew where the steps were leading. As parents we felt like we were walking in the dark.

But at least we were taking our baby home.

JILL: It was a wonderful day when we carried Kirsteen into the house. Her little cot had been sitting there for so long, empty. Every night for five weeks I'd looked at it and thought, she should be here with us. And now she finally was.

It was wonderful to be able to pick her up without that metal bar across her ankles. The difference was incredible. She'd gone from being a patient to being our little baby, just like that. But she was still very delicate.

Try telling that to her brothers though!

They wanted to touch her as soon as we walked through the door, but that's the last thing we could allow to happen. Over the next few weeks they wanted to stroke and cuddle her all the time, but kids can be a bit heavy-handed and we had to keep them away. I felt terrible. They only wanted to show they loved her.

It was worse still when they came running over to cuddle us and we were holding Kirsteen; we were very conscious that she could be hurt and would have to shoo them away. We were only trying to protect her, but imagine how it looked to them.

The boys were so young themselves, and we were such a close, tactile family that they weren't used to that. It was confusing for them. And although we always try to explain things to them, sometimes when they want a cuddle they don't want to listen.

It wasn't just that Kirsteen was so small and weak. It was that her stomach was a particular no-go area, because of the little scars there that needed to heal.

To help us keep her abdomen as clean as possible, we were given petroleum jelly-coated gauze strips. Her tummy was wrapped up like an Egyptian mummy's, but at least it was hygienic. Whenever we changed her nappy, we had to change the gauze. And we'd been told never to let it dry out. Not only would there be an increased risk of germs, but it could also stick to her wounds.

What with keeping the boys away from Kirsteen, and ensuring that her wounds were always protected, it seemed only a matter of time before something went wrong.

And then of course it did, although it wasn't the boys' fault.

Martin had just come home from work. Not wanting to leave all his photographic equipment in the van overnight, he brought it into the house and left it in the hallway while he hung up his coat. Of course, the boys came rushing out with their toys when they heard him and, sidetracked, he picked them up and took them into the lounge.

I'd just finished changing Kirsteen when I heard all the fuss downstairs, so I came trotting down with her. Just as I reached the bottom step, I saw Martin's boxes stacked up. I adjusted my weight quickly to avoid them, but tripped over a toy truck that one of the boys had dropped when their dad came in.

It all happened so quickly. I didn't even have time to scream. I was falling forwards with Kirsteen in my arms, but I managed to turn my body so that I landed back first. I hit the floor with a terrific noise and Martin came rushing out.

'Jill! God, what's happened?'

Being in the police force, Martin knows his first aid. He knew instantly what needed to be done. But I wasn't interested in how hard I'd hit my head. What about little Kirsteen?

'I think she's fine,' Martin said. The shock had made her cry, but she appeared to be moving all right. 'You shielded her,' he said.

'God, think what would have happened if I had—'

He cut me short. 'Let's not think about it.'

I don't drink alcohol but I could really have done with a brandy that night. I was shaking, and not just from the shock of falling. I couldn't stop playing over in my head what would have happened if I'd fallen a different way.

I felt sick thinking about it.

'Hasn't the poor girl suffered enough?' I said to Martin.

He was distraught too, and couldn't apologise enough for leaving his boxes in the hallway. We tried to change the subject, but after a few minutes of chatting about something else, one of us would say, 'What if?' and we'd be crying again.

The next day I was still shaken but I sensed that the feeling was passing. My heart didn't feel like it was going to leap out of my mouth any more and, although I think the guilt will always remain, physically I was calming down. I managed to busy myself with the usual routine of feeds, baths and playtimes with my three beautiful children, and tried to concentrate on things to come, not things that had gone.

It was then that I made a decision about my own life. I realised I had handled this near tragedy pretty well, all things considered. So why was I wasting my time taking antidepressants that only sick people needed? With each day that passed, I reasoned, I was getting mentally stronger and stronger. So I decided there and then that I would stop taking the Seroxat.

What I didn't know was that the effort would very nearly kill me.

CHAPTER 7

I Wanted to Die

KIRSTEEN: When I had my first operation Mr Fyfe made it clear to my parents that it was only the first stage. What frustrated them was the fact he couldn't say how many more stages it might take. He wouldn't even commit to whether I would *ever* be 'cured'.

But while everyone was thinking about me, my mum had problems of her own. Nobody saw it coming. And nobody told her she would be suffering for the rest of her life.

JILL: Everything was going so well at home. We'd got into a bit of a rhythm, juggling Kirsteen's healthcare and making sure the boys got lots of attention as well. Martin was working a fair bit of overtime when he could, so money wasn't as tight, and even though we were both tired I thought it was just a normal part of life with small ones.

We were getting to know a few people through the BEES

group, and knowing there was support out there made us feel a lot more comfortable dealing with everything, so that Kirsteen's condition didn't scare us so much any more. Mr Fyfe had written to us with a date for the next operation, and everything suddenly seemed so straightforward that I felt coming off the tablets was the right thing to do.

It was the biggest mistake of my life. My depression returned with a vengeance and three days later I wanted to kill myself.

I don't know what I was thinking. The kids were in bed and something in my head just snapped. I knew my time was up.

I'm just so lucky Martin came home when he did.

'Jesus, Jill!' he cried.

I can't imagine what he thought. I was lying on the upstairs landing, yelling and swearing and shouting that I wanted to end it. I didn't know how I was going to do it but I knew I wanted the pain in my head to go away. There was only one way that was going to happen. I wanted to die.

I don't know if on some level I'd planned it at a time when Martin was due home. I just know that I hadn't wanted to do anything when the children were around. Even though I wasn't thinking straight, I knew that I had to protect them.

Martin shouted the place down as he tried to restrain me. He is trained to deal with all sorts of troublemakers, so putting me in my place shouldn't have been a problem. But trying to deal with a suicidal wife alters the equation. It must have been awful for him.

He made sure I was under control then reached for the phone. He got through to a doctor and explained what had happened. The doctor told him some stark truths.

'What was your wife thinking stopping the tablets? Wasn't she told she could never come off them? She has to take them for life.'

A forensic pathologist friend of ours phoned up the manufacturers of the tablets and was told something similar – that the tablets are not addictive in the sense that you want to take more and more, but if you want to come off them you have to wean yourself off very, very gradually. If you don't, you'll suffer twice the depression you had beforehand.

It seemed like I was stuck with them.

I was really knocked out by that. 'This isn't how I want to spend my life,' I thought. 'I don't need to take drugs. I've always been so good at coping. Drugs are for sick people. And I'm all right now.'

But that was that. I was told I'd be dependent on them. For ever.

After a while of taking them every day like a good girl I went back to my doctor and said, 'I don't think they're doing anything for me – can I have something else instead?'

'In theory, yes you can,' he said. 'But before you can start another course of treatment you would have to come off these tablets for about a fortnight.'

We both knew that I couldn't do that. Based on my previous experience I'd be dead within the week.

So instead they just doubled my dose. I went in there to get off the stuff, and ended up with twice as much. And as the years have gone by, so my dosage has increased. Recently, now my children are all teenagers, I have started to see a counsellor; perhaps one day I will be able to say goodbye to Seroxat.

The drugs have the effect of making me feel like my emotions have been capped. It takes a lot to tip me over the edge now. I'm totally level. They stop me getting depressed but I'm sure they also suppress everything else. I used to be happier. I know I used to be able to laugh a lot more. But I don't feel that any more. Emotion-wise you just plough this middle furrow.

MARTIN: It's an unnerving way to live, knowing that things could change at any moment. We were always fully aware that Kirsteen would have to go back to Yorkhill, but once you get into the swing of actual day-to-day living you find you haven't really got time to worry too much about the future. It's just a case of getting through today and hoping tomorrow's all right as well.

Just when I felt we were getting the hang of life with three small children aged three and under, things changed.

Kirsteen was about a year old when we got the letter from Mr Fyfe saying that a date had been fixed for her next operation. When I read it I felt like I was going back in time. All my initial fears came flooding back. The thought of my little girl going back in there was horrible.

Jill and I had done a pretty decent job of not worrying each other about Kirsteen up to that point. But now we were reminded of just how fragile she was.

What's her quality of life going to be like? I wondered. Will she ever live a normal life? And the awful thing was that even after I'd spoken to Mr Fyfe, I still didn't know the answers.

When Kirsteen had had her first operation just hours after she was born, I think I'd been in too much of a state of shock to register the enormity of it all.

Taking her back in now, seemed worse, somehow. All my fears were heightened. What if it didn't work? What if something went wrong? What if they couldn't fix her?

And, worst of all: what if she didn't wake up?

We were only allowed as far as the room where the general anaesthetic was administered. Seeing a cable fitted to a little socket called a cannula in her hand was hard to stomach. But watching her go under as the drug took its grip was totally traumatic.

One minute she was there, a little wriggling, crying, quite naturally distressed baby. She looked tiny and fragile then, but she was noisy and very much alive. But seconds later, she looked completely different. She'd gone from being a wonderful babbling baby to being limp, unconscious, like a little rag doll. It was terrifying.

I found it hard enough to witness as it was. But what made the experience more painful was recalling what Jill had explained to me a few days earlier.

'The anaesthetic is the most dangerous part of the operation,' she told me. 'One tiny miscalculation and somebody could die.'

I wish she hadn't said that, but it helped me to appreciate what a skilled job – and what a risky one – it was. If the dose was too small, the patient could wake up during surgery and feel the pain, but be unable to cry out; if it was too great, there was a real threat of brain damage – or death.

Mr Fyfe's original words to us came flashing back into my mind. 'Don't worry, it's not life-threatening,' he'd said. He was talking about Kirsteen's condition. But could he honestly say the same of each operation?

I studied the expression on the anaesthetist's face as Kirsteen went under and her body flopped on to the little bed. He seemed perfectly satisfied. I tried to take comfort from that, but it was hard.

Jill and I held each other for dear life. We wanted to be

strong because there was nothing else we could do. But it was easier said than done.

A few moments later, two nurses in theatre scrubs each grabbed a side of the bed and pushed it through a pair of large swing doors, and Kirsteen disappeared into theatre. We were sent back through another door and into the ward. All we could do was wait.

And wait.

The aim of the operation was to protect Kirsteen's kidneys. Mr Fyfe was worried about the possibility of reflux, which can cause severe kidney damage and, in the long term, can be catastrophic. I think they felt that the original drainage system they had put in place was not working properly, making reflux a serious concern.

Mr Fyfe explained the process to us. 'We'll be inserting what is known as a suprapubic catheter into Kirsteen and sewing it into her bladder,' he said. 'To look at, it is a rubber tube that comes out about six or eight inches and has one wide end on it. We expect the urine to flow through this tube, out of her body and straight into a nappy.'

I can't say I was thrilled at the thought of a tube poking out of the side of Kirsteen's stomach. He made it sound like a dripping tap. But if I was less than impressed by this, I was positively disenchanted with the answer to another question.

'Mr Fyfe,' I asked. 'Can you tell us where this features in your plans for Kirsteen in the long term?'

He looked at me and said, 'Well, how long's a piece of string?' From the tone of his voice I got the distinct impression that the subject was closed. If he had what I would call a 'proper' answer, he wasn't prepared to share it with us.

If I hadn't been so worried about Kirsteen I would have taken him to task. But when you're talking to the man who will be operating on your daughter, you think differently. You go with the flow. If the consultant tells you he wants to try this, or test that, but doesn't explain things fully, you have to trust him. He knows more than you do.

But I remember feeling distinctly uneasy.

It was another marathon waiting session while the surgeons carried out their work. When Kirsteen was brought back out I was so relieved to see her that I didn't really have the strength to question our consultant further. He seemed pleased with the way things had gone, however, and said Kirsteen should be noticing the difference soon.

He was right – but not in the way we expected.

Babies may not be able to talk to you, but they do get their message across. Every father knows his own baby. Every mother too. Whatever anyone else says, you know when they're not well.

It was a couple of days after Kirsteen's operation. We'd been allowed to take her home, but Jill and I could both see she was distressed. Her stomach was obviously very sensitive because of the surgery, but I knew her pain was to do with more than just her new scars. It was obvious she was in severe discomfort. The doctors had said that it might take a short while for the effects of the operation to settle down, but how much more of this could Kirsteen take?

Every position we put her in seemed to upset her more. She screamed if she was flat and she screamed if we picked her up. We were at our wits' end.

Then I said, 'What about the car seat?' At least in that she would be upright and quite restricted in her movement so she couldn't hurt herself. So, for the next week Kirsteen pretty much lived in that seat.

Still, we were seriously worried that the healing wasn't going to plan. And when pus started to seep from Kirsteen's stomach we knew something was definitely wrong. We agreed that we would have to take her back to Yorkhill.

Mr Fyfe agreed that something wasn't working and said that they would operate immediately.

For the second time in a fortnight, Jill and I found ourselves standing in that small, sterile anteroom, looking on as the anaesthetist attached a cannula to Kirsteen's hand. I flinched as the needle went in, and felt my stomach leap when Kirsteen slumped.

'That doesn't get any easier to watch,' I said.

'It never will,' Jill agreed.

'I just hope we don't have to see it too many times,' I said. But I think we both knew that was plain wishful thinking.

I was worried about what the surgeons would find when they operated on Kirsteen this time, given that whatever they had tried to do last time seemed not to have worked. Would they attempt the same procedure again and hope for better results? Or would they take an alternative tack?

From the anxious parents' point of view, it almost felt like our daughter was being treated like a guinea pig. But we had to have faith in her doctors. They were the only chance she stood of a healthy life.

When Kirsteen was brought out again my heart sank. In order to quell the pain caused by the suprapubic catheter, Mr Fyfe had brought Kirsteen's bladder back to the surface again. She looked just as she had on the day she was born. I couldn't believe it; we seemed to have gone full circle. But at least she didn't seem to be in any discomfort.

I wish I could have said the same for Jill and me.

Our job as parents had suddenly become harder. Kirsteen was already a delicate baby, but now we had to ensure that her external bladder was protected at all times. To the doctors and nurses, I'm sure it must have all seemed fairly straightforward. But we had no experience of caring for someone with such a fragile appendage. Jill, I have to say, was marvellous at coping, but I was very concerned that we were expected to look after Kirsteen in this condition with no external medical help.

We had to monitor her bladder hourly, ensuring that it was always kept damp with petroleum gauze bandages. It seeped urine continuously, which had nowhere to go apart from directly onto her skin. The gel was the only protection against this; without it Kirsteen would eventually burn herself as well as risk infection. She withstood it very well, but I'm sure it must have been very unpleasant for her.

'I think it looks worse than it is,' Jill said.

We both hoped that was true.

For a few weeks our lives were, once again, turned on their heads. Kirsteen's hourly changes didn't stop just because it was night-time. At least in hospital we'd had nurses on night shift who could take over. At home, we were on our own.

After the first night, Jill and I were both like zombies. She was too tired to look after the kids that day, and I was a mess as I tried to keep my eyes open at work. If we were going to keep this up, we needed a system. After a couple of different patterns, we decided that I would do a lot of the early changes and Jill would do as many as she could in the night. That way, at least, we both got a block of sleep, even if it was only four hours.

It always amazes me how quickly the human body adapts. That sleep pattern went on for several months, and before we knew it, we were waking up before the alarm clock went off. I might have looked like death, but I was managing to juggle work and home. That was as much as I could ask for. You sort of switch to autopilot mode. It's the only way to cope.

Keeping the boys away from Kirsteen became an even greater priority when she was in this state. For as long as the smallest little hand could seriously damage her, we had to limit all fraternal cuddles and interaction. Kenneth could sense that something was wrong, but obviously didn't know what. All he knew was that he wasn't allowed near his little sister again.

It really did seem like we'd wound the clock back to the bad old days.

JILL: We were always confident in the measures that Yorkhill was taking, and felt sure that Kirsteen was in the best hands, but both Martin and I felt that we could have been better informed.

We decided that we needed to make greater efforts to maintain contact with the BEES network. Hopefully, talking to other sufferers would give us all the answers we required.

We learned that the support group's annual general meeting would be taking place a few months later down in London, at Great Ormond Street Children's Hospital. I remembered reading that J. M. Barrie had given them the rights to his children's story, Peter Pan, earning them millions of pounds every year. But I didn't really have any idea about the work they did there.

As soon as he got the chance, Martin called the BEES chairwoman, a lady called Jane Wallace; we were desperate to get along to the AGM to learn as much as we could. Chatting to Jane, Martin learned that she had a twelve-year-old daughter, Inya, who was born with bladder exstrophy (which is why she'd got so involved with the group). He asked her about the meeting at Great Ormond Street, and happened to mention that it was scheduled for after our summer holiday.

'That's funny,' Jane said. 'We're going on holiday to Scotland.'

'Really?' Martin said. 'Whereabouts?'

'It's a little island called Iona.'

Martin was stunned. Our holiday was booked for the Isle of Mull – the very next island. And the coincidences didn't stop there. It turned out that we would all be travelling on exactly the same day – and that we were booked on to the same ferry, which stops at both islands.

'There's got to be a reason for this,' I said when Martin told me.

We couldn't wait for the holiday to come round. It was something for us to look forward to after the time we'd had recently. And it wasn't just Kirsteen's latest operations that had been taking their toll.

It had been bound to happen sooner or later. I knew that. And, sure enough, the day came when we were all invited to a family function at which I knew my mother would be one of the guests.

We discussed not going, but decided it would not be fair on the children to keep them from the rest of their relatives. There was no reason to punish them.

I refused to let myself get too worked up about it. It had been the same with my mother all my life. She never changed when I was growing up, and she hadn't done since

I'd been an adult. The fact that I hadn't seen her for so many months didn't surprise me. It made me sad, but I think I was sad for her. 'Look what she's missing out on,' I said as I cuddled little Kirsteen.

In the event, we had a nice day. My mother pretended nothing had happened. She was polite to Martin and seemed to have forgotten the whole Erskine Bridge episode. But what I was really worried about was how she'd treat my little girl.

I shouldn't have worried. In front of other members of the family she picked Kirsteen up and treated her like any other grandmother might treat her youngest grandchild.

It was only afterwards that she reverted to type.

'You should sue that hospital,' she said.

'Why?' I asked her. 'There's nothing they could have done to stop it.'

'They should have picked it up on the scans. You had enough of them.'

'What does it matter?' I asked. She was already infuriating me. 'I told you, they couldn't have done anything even if we had known.'

'But at least you would have had a choice.'

And I suddenly understood what she was saying.

'The only choice I would have had would have been whether to ask for a termination,' I said slowly.

She said nothing; she didn't need to.

I realised she hadn't changed a bit. Her words from my childhood came flooding back.

'They should have been dropped on their head when they were born. What's the point in keeping them alive?'

CHAPTER 8

Enough's Enough

KIRSTEEN: Before I was even two years old I'd had six operations. I still have the scars from each one. One of my earliest memories is of being in Yorkhill and thinking, 'Will this be the last time?' I know Mum and Dad were as much in the dark as I was. But they were doing their very best to discover as much as they could about my condition.

MARTIN: Scotland is a wonderfully diverse country. You have the big cities like Glasgow, Edinburgh and Aberdeen, but there are also beautiful mountains and islands and vast expanses of countryside. I love getting away to the islands. We often take our summer holidays on one of these little outposts dotted around the coast and they are always something for the whole family to get excited about.

This time was no different, and as we counted down the days to our next trip to Mull, I realised that we were looking forward to the journey more than ever.

I couldn't get over the coincidence of Jane Wallace being booked on the same ferry as us. It was such a random slice of good fortune – but I suppose we were due a bit of good luck after all this time. The last time I'd experienced such a coincidence was the day Kirsteen was born; I've never really come to terms with the fact I'd happened to catch that programme on bladder exstrophy the night before. I hoped this coincidence would have a happier outcome.

Gilbert came along with us on that holiday, which gave us another reason to look forward to it. He had a great affection for the sea after his days with the mobile dental surgery, but he would have gone anywhere just to spend time with the boys and Kirsteen, whom he adored. We thought that the fresh air could only be good for his health problems, and that a week away from his wife would not have done him any harm, either.

As we joined the queue onto the Caledonian MacBrayne car ferry at Oban, we discussed whether Jane Wallace and her family would actually be there. It all seemed too good to be true – something was bound to go wrong.

We piled out of the car and made our way to the cafeteria. One adult to each child just about made it an achievable operation. The boys, of course, wanted to watch the ship move through the water so I said we could give them a few minutes but then we'd have to go.

'I'll look after them if you want to run along,' Gilbert said. It was such a relief having him there.

We were just taking our seats in the cafeteria when Jill spotted another family.

'It's them,' she said.

At the same moment Jane Wallace spotted us. Somehow we instinctively all recognised each other.

Our plan was to catch the ferry to Craignure in Mull while the Wallaces continued on to Iona, then we would hook up with them for a day later in the holiday. You never know for sure how these meetings with strangers are going to go, but from the few minutes I'd spent with Jane on the phone, I was pretty confident we'd all get on.

And I was right. Our two families got on well on the boat ride over, then we all had a terrific day on Iona when we met up again a few days later. Jane's daughter Inya took an instant liking to Kirsteen and she reciprocated. Gilbert talked and played with the boys, while the rest of us shared our experiences.

We heard a lot of stories from Jane. Many were uplifting, but one stayed in my memory for the opposite reason. Jane said that through her role in BEES she heard of a little boy born with bladder exstrophy. Like us, his parents had no idea anything was wrong until he popped out. They were professional people, quite well-to-do, but they took one look at him and decided they couldn't cope. They said to the doctors, 'We can't do it. We can't look after a disabled baby.'

And they just left him there.

Jane told us that when she'd heard about this, she'd gone to the hospital and sat by the side of that little boy's cot every day for weeks, just like his mother should have done.

Jill was in tears when Jane finished the story. Perhaps it affected us so much because we both knew that if her own mother had had her way, we'd have done the same thing with Kirsteen.

The whole point of a holiday is to give yourself a break from the humdrum nature of reality, but often you don't really achieve that. On this trip though, I felt a tangible sense of relief.

Jane was an open and decent person, right from the start, and we felt an immediate bond with her. More than fifteen years later, I'm happy to say she remains one of our closest friends.

One of the things that Jane couldn't emphasise enough was the importance the Great Ormond Street meeting.

'You need to get yourselves down there one way or another,' she told us. 'They do such amazing things at that hospital. You need to see it for yourself.'

Jill and I were bowled over by all this talk of London and the treatments available there. But, most of all, Jane had given us hope – for the first time since she'd been born, we thought that Kirsteen might, one day, lead a normal life.

'There is life after bladder exstrophy,' Jane said, 'and a good quality of life at that.'

I'd never dared think that before, but young Inya was living proof.

For the rest of our holiday we were buzzing. The trip to London couldn't come soon enough.

'Do you really think Kirsteen will be mended like Jane's daughter?' Gilbert asked me.

'I don't see why not,' I said. And with another date at Yorkhill around the corner I hoped that possibility was that much closer.

The next step in Mr Fyfe's plan was to reinstate Kirsteen's bladder. It didn't seem to be causing her any pain on the outside, but Jill and I were nervous as kittens with it there. Of course, the hourly changes wouldn't be missed either. You've got to be careful about germs with any child, but with Kirsteen everything had to be spotless. It was pretty exhausting.

The aim of the operation was to install an indwelling catheter. With this in place, Kirsteen's urine would pass through the catheter into a collection bag rather than a nappy. We had our fingers crossed that this one would work, but the sense of dread with which I'd been filled the first time Kirsteen went under the surgeon's knife was as strong on every return visit. And I will never be comfortable watching anyone fall under anaesthetic for as long as I live.

But at least we were used to the waiting. One of the worst aspects of hospital life is the hanging around. You feel so ineffectual, so impotent. It doesn't matter if you're the patient's wife, father or son – you're just a member of the audience once you enter the medical world. You have no part to play other than to watch.

Once more, we were relieved to see the ward doors swing open and the nurses wheel Kirsteen in. But my relief on this occasion was tempered by concern. Kirsteen appeared to have a large drainage bag taped to her little ankle. It looked far too big for her, and I couldn't understand what had been done. I needed to speak to our consultant.

Mr Fyfe assured me that the drainage bag was not as horrific as it seemed. It was not a permanent measure – which was just as well, because she was very difficult to pick up as she was. The external bag needed to stay in place until the catheter was up to speed. The only drawback was we didn't know when that would be.

When Kirsteen was first diagnosed, Mr Fyfe had mentioned that when she was four, she would undergo a procedure called a Mitrofanoff. This, we were led to believe, could be the last step on her journey. Looking at her now, at not even two years old, I found it hard to believe we were even close to the finish line.

By the time our visit to Great Ormond Street Hospital

came around, Jill and I were keen to see if it would live up to the rapturous reviews that Jane Wallace and other members of BEES had given it.

We took the sleeper train down, often the least expensive ticket, but by no means cheap. So, by the time we entered the hospital, we'd already spent more money than we had during our entire week away in Mull. Evidently, treatment in London must be a privilege for the wealthy, we thought.

From the moment we entered the hospital it felt different from Yorkhill. We knew that it was called a children's hospital, but we could never have imagined the lengths to which they go there to make their young patients feel as comfortable as possible. The staff all seemed to be smiling, there were children's paintings on the walls and there wasn't that sense of gloom that hits you when you step inside other hospitals.

The meeting was held in one of the conference rooms. A lot of the parents there clearly already knew each other, and we did our best to introduce ourselves to as many people as we could. Seeing Jane again was a particular treat, and she made sure we felt at ease. One of the speakers told us about a ward at Great Ormond Street – the Louise Ward – which is an area specifically for children with bladder exstrophy. I struggled to process what I was hearing.

'Can you believe that?' I nudged Jill. 'They have a ward dedicated to bladder exstrophy.'

'Martin, we've got to get Kirsteen here,' she said.

I made a mental note to approach Mr Fyfe on our return.

The main speaker at the meeting only reinforced our admiration for the hospital. Mr Philip Ransley was the leading consultant in charge of bladder exstrophy cases. He explained how the Louise Ward always had several patients so the condition was being treated at all times. Every new development was monitored and the latest theories were taken on board. Mr Ransley was certainly an impressive man to listen to, and he was backed by an enviable array of resources. What really impressed me, however, was his manner. He explained more about bladder exstrophy in a twenty-minute speech than I'd managed to glean in two years from the staff at Yorkhill.

This was the man I wanted to be in charge of my daughter's health, I decided.

For the remainder of our visit, we were given a tour of the hospital's wards and further opportunities to mingle with other sufferers and their families. Considering that every person in the room had been touched to a greater or lesser extent by the same disability, there was an overwhelmingly upbeat atmosphere. And Jill and I were no different. As we made the journey back home to Glasgow, we were both convinced of what had to be done.

It was with some trepidation that I made the appointment to see Alasdair Fyfe. As a policeman, I'm used to dealing with unpleasant assignments, but straight talking on a personal level is always that much harder.

We sat down in Mr Fyfe's office.

'What's on your mind, Mr Lupton?'

I explained about our trip. 'I'm finding this very hard to put to you, and I'm not decrying you in any way, shape or form, but we've been to Great Ormond Street to a support-group meeting.' Then I rattled off some details about BEES and what we'd seen.

'Well, I'd be wary of these support groups,' he said. 'No two cases are the same.'

Fair enough, I thought, and continued, 'We have seen the

facilities they have there for treating bladder exstrophy. And I'm just wondering, would you happen to know, is there anything you would say that they can offer Kirsteen at Great Ormond Street that you can't do for her here at Yorkhill?'

I'd finally got the question out into the open. I could relax.

'I'm very, very glad you felt able to ask me that,' Mr Fyfe said. 'I'm not a proud man, and of course you want the best for your daughter. But what I'll say to you is this: I know the team down at Great Ormond Street well – we meet up regularly – and if I thought there was one thing they could do for your daughter that I wouldn't tackle, I would have no hesitation in sending you there.'

Well, you can't say fairer than that, I thought. A refreshingly honest answer.

I relayed everything to Jill, and together we decided that we'd let the treatment at Yorkhill run its course. We were very wary of the upheaval of taking the family down to London, and we now had renewed confidence that the care Kirsteen would get in Glasgow would be as effective as that in Great Ormond Street. A date was pencilled in for Kirsteen's Mitrofanoff procedure. Things were looking up.

Sadly, as it turned out, however, someone very special would not be around to see it.

Kirsteen was in hospital for treatment over the Easter weekend of 1995, and I alternated my time between being at her bedside and keeping the boys entertained in the ward's day room. Jill, however, had to split her time between Kirsteen and her father who had been admitted to another hospital near by. Gilbert had been suffering from chest complaints and circulation problems in his legs for some time, and he had finally gone in to have his arteries replaced.

After seeing him the day before Jill had reported that the operation seemed to have been successful and that the doctors were very happy with him. So the news that something had gone wrong came completely out of the blue.

It was Suzanne who called and told us that Gilbert wasn't expected to last the day. 'He's got some sort of infection,' she explained. We prayed for the doctors to be wrong, but, on this occasion, they weren't. The only good thing was that Jill was at his side when he died.

By the time Jill called me with the news, I had taken the boys home from visiting their little sister. The phone rang just after teatime.

'It's Dad,' Jill said. 'He's gone.'

Dealing with the death of her wonderful father was yet another burden for Jill. It was for all of us, of course. We all loved him. But Jill was torn between being with her siblings and spending time as usual with Kirsteen. I was very worried about her. We rarely spoke about her dependency on antidepressants, but at that time I was glad she had them. How much more was one person expected to put up with?

And then there were the boys. They probably felt more out of it than ever. Kirsteen was really bad, in so much pain, they'd lost their grandfather and Jill was in a terrible way. She was bursting into tears at the drop of a hat, and that must have scared them.

'If Mummy cries when she's with you, it's not your fault,' I told them. But you could see in their eyes that they didn't know what to think.

They were growing at a furious rate at this time. I don't know where the time went, but before I knew it Kenneth and Martin were both at school. It's a proud day when you first watch your little ones go through the school gates on their own. At the same time, though, we knew there were no guarantees that we'd ever have the same experience with Kirsteen.

She'd been a naturally small baby and she was growing into a slight little girl. All the trips to hospital had held her back physically and her growth didn't seem to be on the same chart as other kids. While the boys were crawling all over the place at around six to eight months, Kirsteen was still unable to roll over. We were assured she would catch up, but those long stretches in hospital had taken valuable months off her development.

As for walking, it seemed like a pipe dream. All children blossom at their own pace and the last thing you want is to be pushy. On the other hand, we were trying so hard to give Kirsteen as normal a life as we could manage. We started to worry seriously about this when she was eighteen months old and were referred to the Achamore Centre in Drumchapel for some physiotherapy sessions.

When Kirsteen first started to pull herself up and stand on her own two feet, these were incredible milestones. I couldn't wait for those first shaky steps – but yet another cloud hung over her. We were told by various doctors that children who have undergone an operation to reset the pubic bone might never walk as comfortably as others. One of the possible side effects is a wider gait.

This was always at the back of our minds as we waited for the day that Kirsteen would finally take her first steps. In the event, when the time came, I was so thrilled that I don't think I thought about her gait once, and to this day, if she has got a slightly wider stride, it's so marginal I don't think anyone would notice.

As much as we were desperate for Kirsteen to one day achieve a normal quality of life, I was never happier than when she was wrapped up in the little cocoon we created for her at home. It seemed to me that there were so many potential problems once you stepped out the front door, especially now that the boys were in school.

To Kenneth and Martin, Kirsteen was just their little sister. But as they started to get to know other boys and girls they would soon learn she was different. We've always been very honest with our children, and told them as much as possible. But even so, there was a lot of responsibility on those young shoulders.

'What if the other boys take the mickey out of them because of Kirsteen?' Jill worried.

'If I know our lads they'll only do it once,' I said.

But I couldn't be sure. I know what kids are like. They don't take to anything out of the ordinary and the last thing we wanted was Kenneth and Martin picked on because of their sister. What if it made them think differently about Kirsteen? Sometimes after a trip to hospital she had to be pushed around in a wheelchair. You could sense a dozen kids staring when we dropped the boys off at class with her in tow. What if Kenneth and Martin started to look at her differently?

It was Jill's turn to reassure me. 'That will never happen,' she said. 'And if it does, we'll deal with it then.'

We were so anxious not to make our family stand out that I think in the early days we actually lost sight of the bigger picture, and it turned out that in trying to help the boys fit in, we actually made them feel more alienated. When they started school, we made a decision not to tell their teachers anything about their sister that they didn't need to know.

But, looking back, it's clear that we should have been more upfront.

Martin hadn't long been at school when Kirsteen went into hospital for an operation. We were so wrapped up in worrying about her that we didn't think to tell Kenneth's and Martin's teachers that the boys might be affected by what was happening. When I picked the lads up the day after the operation, they each handed me a note. 'Kenneth was terribly upset today but I couldn't find out why,' said one of them. 'Martin wasn't himself today. Is everything all right at home?' asked the other.

I felt so guilty.

'We've really taken our eye off the ball here,' I said to Jill.

The next day I went into the school and made a full disclosure. If there was any more fallout, at least the teachers would know what they were dealing with.

Despite whatever we may have said to the boys, being among so many 'normal' families on a day-to-day basis does highlight your differences. Even Jill and I felt that. It also exacerbates your fears. Like any other parents, we worried about what the future had in store for our children, but with Kirsteen our targets had to be different. We were always primed for her next surgical procedure. It was hard to look much further ahead than that.

The date for the Mitrofanoff procedure came along quicker than we expected. It's incredible how time flies when you're embroiled in the domestic chaos of everyday life.

It was September 1997, just a few weeks shy of Kirsteen's fourth birthday when we returned to Yorkhill again, and, for the first time since she was born, we felt there was light at the end of the tunnel.

'Do you honestly think this will be the end?' Jill said.

'I hope so, I really do,' I replied. 'I don't know how much more of this we can put her through.'

As it was explained to me, the Mitrofanoff procedure was the most ambitious piece of surgery Kirsteen had undergone to date. In fact, Mr Fyfe said he would be working alongside another surgeon. 'Two heads are better than one,' he told me.

The point of the operation was to use the appendix to create a channel from the abdomen into the bladder, through which a catheter could be inserted to empty the bladder of urine, bypassing the urethra. A stoma – which works a bit like a valve but looks like an extra belly button – sits on the surface of the tummy and the catheter is inserted through there. The idea is to give the patient some control over their life. In theory, if it was successful, Kirsteen would be able to insert a disposable catheter into her stoma and syphon or drain her urine. She would have to do this every four hours for the rest of her life. But at least she would be in charge of her own body for the first time. At least she would be able to come out of nappies at the age of four. At least she would be dry.

As the hours passed while Kirsteen was in theatre, we mulled over how life would change for us. Not having to change her little nappies would make a huge difference to the quality of both her life and ours. I didn't quite comprehend what this new method of draining through a spare tummy button really involved, but it sounded better than our current system.

Jill and I told ourselves to remain calm, but it was impossible. We couldn't wait to see the change when she came out. We weren't expecting miracles, but just to see our little girl out of nappies would really enrich our lives.

When the surgery team finally emerged, I could tell they seemed satisfied with the way things had gone.

The stoma, which looked like a little peeled cherry tomato coming out of her body, was very raw, very exposed. It was not dissimilar to how her bladder had looked. My heart sank when I saw it. I could foresee just how careful we would have to be with this arrangement, and any hope we may have had of Kirsteen having a semblance of normal childhood looked as far off as ever. But at least an end to the reliance on nappies was in sight.

But things didn't go as planned, and within hours of Kirsteen waking up, we realised something had gone very wrong.

The first sign we had was the most heart-wrenching. Kirsteen was obviously in enormous pain but it wasn't apparent at first, at least to us, what was causing it. She struggled like mad as a doctor tried to apply the disposable catheter and I thought her screams would bring the walls down. When he finally succeeded that should have been the end. But it was soon clear that something was leaking severely.

During the operation, the urethra – the part which actually passes urine from the body – was supposed to have been completely closed off so nothing could pass through. This hadn't worked.

I felt as though I was watching my world fall apart. I think if I'd been alone I would have crumbled. As it was, I felt so deflated, and so sorry for Kirsteen. Another operation, another general anaesthetic, and we seemed no closer to a resolution for her than before.

Mr Fyfe explained why he thought it had gone wrong. I understood his explanation to be that because the urethra had never passed anything before, it was too small for him to find or close off properly. He had not believed it would be an issue.

Jill and I looked at each other. There were no words. What could we say?

Kirsteen spent her fourth birthday in hospital. We tried to be upbeat but it was a difficult act to pull off. Our daughter was four years old, still in nappies and suffering a lot of pain because her bladder wasn't large enough to last for four hours without draining. She needed to be catheterised every ninety minutes, twenty-four hours a day, which meant she was always tired. She was worse off than she had ever been.

We remembered what Jane Wallace had said about a decent quality of life and thought just how far off from that Kirsteen still seemed to be.

Towards the end of her stay Mr Fyfe told us that he would be bringing Kirsteen back into surgery in a few months to try to locate and close her urethra. He made it clear that this was not a minor procedure. 'I should warn you there's around a fifty to sixty per cent chance of pulling it off,' he told us.

Jill and I thought of Kirsteen lying there in bed and knew what we had to do.

'Enough's enough,' I said to Jill as soon as Dr Fyfe was gone. 'We're taking her to Great Ormond Street.'

CHAPTER 9

You're Killing Her

KIRSTEEN: Most of my early memories are associated with my illness. One of my first is of asking my doctor at Yorkhill, Mr Fyfe, how long I'd be in hospital for. I didn't like hospital because I was always unwell there. For me it meant being in pain. And I remember clearly him saying, 'How long is a piece of string?'

I was three at the time.

That's my only memory of Yorkhill.

I never felt different from anyone else or out of the ordinary because this was all I knew. I had always been ill. That was normal for me. It was just the way I was. I never looked at my mum and dad or my brothers and thought, 'You're normal – and I'm not.' I knew that there was something wrong with my tummy because I had always been told not to bash my stomach. I remember thinking, 'Why are my brothers allowed to roll over onto their stomachs and

I'm not? Why can't I do that? Why can't I do what they're doing?'

I put it down to other things, like being younger than them, or being a girl. I can't honestly say I put it down to being ill.

Mum and Dad always explained everything to me as much as they could. There was only ever one thing they held back, which was when I was due to have my next operation. They usually didn't tell me about my hospital appointments until the day before, partly because they didn't want me to worry, but also because they knew I would fight against it.

I hated the idea of going back to hospital. Mum and Dad would say things like, 'It's for your own good' or 'It will make you better', but that doesn't have much of an impact when you're three or four. All I could think about was how unhappy I was every time I went in, and how painful it always was.

I hated everything about the operations. I didn't like the smell of them, I didn't like how every room in the hospital looked the same, and I hated the thought of them because whenever I woke up I just felt more ill. I remember thinking, 'Why are they doing this to me again?' It's hard to understand when you're young.

The worst times were always straight after operations. I would always think, 'If they're trying to make me better, why do I always feel so much worse after they've done something to me?' After my Mitrofanoff it felt like my stomach was going to explode. I remember waking up once and thinking I was going to die because of the pain. I couldn't move. I was screaming, 'I'm going to burst!' Mum and Dad had to help sit me up, but all the while it felt like I had stomach cramps and they were going to split my tummy.

Is it any wonder I hated going back in?

So I suppose it was probably easier for everyone if I was told about the next round at the last minute, so I didn't have time to argue. At most it was a one-day fight and by then I couldn't do anything about it anyway.

I think sometimes people are surprised that sick people have any spirit. I remember some friends of my parents looking at me as though I might crack. Because my body was quite frail, I don't think they expected me to have any opinions of my own. But one of the things my parents have always done is to treat me just like my brothers as much as they could. So from an early age I was as much trouble as they were. And the thing I hated most as a little girl was being told what to do, even if it was for my own good. I don't think I'm much better now!

JILL: I couldn't wait to get Kirsteen home after the Mitrofanoff procedure. I just felt we could all do with time away from the hospital. Me, Martin, Kirsteen, the whole family. The downside, though, was we had to learn how to 'plug in' a catheter and drain her.

The nurses at the hospital made it look so straight-forward. The advantage they had over us was that they could be more matter-of-fact about the pain it obviously caused Kirsteen. They knew it was for her own good and they had to get on with it. It was their job. But Martin and I felt every wince. When you have to do something that makes your own child scream, it's worse than if you're hurting yourself.

But once they'd shown us how to insert the catheter at Yorkhill, we left. We were on our own.

Martin's parents were staying with us that week. They'd come up to see Kirsteen in hospital, but by the time they arrived she had been discharged. I thought the extra pairs of hands would be a great help; instead it was just another pair of worrying heads.

When it came to doing the first catheter at home I couldn't believe how tense I was. We had everything ready – the Vaseline, the gauze, the fresh nappy and the catheter. You had to be so organised, especially remembering to keep the faeces and the urine totally separated. Nothing was allowed to contaminate the stomach area and things like talcum powder were definitely off limits. The stoma had to remain clean and lubricated at all times. The preparation was stressful enough in itself, but now we had to begin the procedure.

We must have projected our own nervousness on to Kirsteen. She wriggled like mad and Martin had to hold her down.

'Let me go!' she was shouting. 'It hurts.'

We hadn't even started yet.

I prepared her tummy and changed her nappy. I had the catheter ready – all I needed to do now was go through with it.

'Come on, Jill, take a deep breath and go for it,' Martin said.

I can still picture Kirsteen's face now, contorted in agony as I tried to insert the catheter. And I can definitely hear her screams. I twisted and I pushed, but I could not get that tube inside her. Something was making it stick. With every attempt I made, Kirsteen cried louder and louder.

Martin's mother was the first to crack.

'Are you sure you're doing it right?' she asked through her own tears.

'I'm doing what I was shown!' I shouted.

We were all distraught. But it had to be done. Time was ticking by. I couldn't afford for her bladder to overfill and leak inside.

'I can't watch any more of this,' my mother-in-law said, and left the room.

With every second that passed, Kirsteen screamed more and more.

It was a nightmare scene. I still sometimes wake up at night in a sweat remembering it.

Suddenly, there was a crash and the door flew open. Young Martin was standing there, ashen. Tears were streaming down his face.

'Stop it!' he screamed at me. 'You're killing her!'

That must have been what it looked and sounded like to him.

'Stop it!' he screamed again. 'Call an ambulance!' He was panicking now. 'I'm going to call the police!' Then fled out of the room.

I wanted to go after him but we had to get the catheter attached.

I heard Martin's mum try to calm him down. Thank goodness they were there. It's at just such times of crisis that you need help.

After about ten minutes we got the catheter in. That wasn't the end of Kirsteen's tears, but at least we could see the catheter drain her bladder.

'Well, we did it,' Martin said.

I nodded, exhausted.

'I don't think I can go through that again,' I said.

But we both knew there was no choice. And the next time would be less than two hours later.

The operation should have allowed Kirsteen the freedom to drain her urine every four hours during the day, and less frequently at night. Because it had gone wrong, for a few weeks we had to do it every ninety minutes. Catheterising for the rest of her life was the best Kirsteen could hope for but at the moment even that didn't look straightforward. Each time we thought we were close to escaping the tiring treadmill, it kept drawing us in.

We were now more determined than ever to explore other avenues. We didn't know for sure that Great Ormond Street held all the answers – but we knew we had to see.

The problem was we had to get through a lot of red tape first. The politics are complicated. Each part of the country is given a health service allowance. You can't just pick and choose where you go for treatment, and unless you pay for private healthcare, you have to go to your nearest hospital. The normal way around it is a referral from your hospital, but they have to agree to this.

Yorkhill refused.

'What are we going to do now?' I said to Martin. 'We can't afford to pay to go down to London.'

I was advised to see our GP. We explained our case to Dr Kent who agreed to write to the local health board to see if they would be willing to fund Kirsteen's stay at Great Ormond Street.

'It's a specialist hospital and Kirsteen needs specialist treatment,' he explained to us. 'I think you have a very good case.'

Even so, the wait until we heard back was tortuous.

Weeks went by and then we received a letter from the health board. My fingers barely worked as I scrabbled at the paper to see what the verdict was.

Yes! I couldn't wait to call Martin at work and tell him. 'They said yes!'

Once the funding was agreed, we still had to get an appointment. As with any National Health Service organisation, this was not quick. In fact the earliest date they could give us was still several months away. It was hard, but at least we had something to look forward to.

In the meantime, we had to continue with Kirsteen's round-the-clock care – and also prepare her for starting school. But just keeping her out of trouble wasn't that straightforward, not if we wanted her to live a normal life.

We've always encouraged the kids to have friends round. Maybe it's a reaction to my own upbringing, when my mother would never allow me to have anybody over, let alone to stay, but our house now is constantly full of people. Guy Fawkes, for example, has always been a big event for us since we've had children. Every year we have about sixty people over for a barbecue, adults and children; everyone just crashes where they can.

One reason for this is to give the children another date in the calendar to look forward to. But there's another reason. I'd rather be run off my feet with a full house than worrying about where anyone is and what they're getting up to. At least under my own roof I can keep an eye on things. Unfortunately, however, I don't have X-ray vision and every so often something slips through.

I was in the kitchen one day, when Kirsteen was about five years old, and she was playing upstairs with her friend Hannah. I'd checked on them about five minutes earlier and they'd been happily sorting through Kirsteen's doll collection.

The next thing I heard was, 'Aaaagh!'

It was a blood-curdling scream, straight out of a horror movie. I rushed into the hallway and there was Hannah, hysterical with fright and pointing at Kirsteen.

With my heart in my mouth, I looked quickly over at my daughter. Her T-shirt was soaked through with blood.

My head was spinning. 'What have you done? What's wrong?' I couldn't get any sense out of either of them.

'Kirsteen,' I shouted. 'Tell me what's happened. Are you hurt?'

I soon realised that Kirsteen was the only one out of the three of us who was not hysterical. And then she told me what had happened.

KIRSTEEN: One minute Hannah and I were playing with my dolls, the next we were talking about sliding down the stairs on our tummies. I'd never done that before so I couldn't wait to try it. We threw the dolls down and lined up next to each other on our fronts at the top of the stairs.

I don't remember thinking, 'This will be dangerous.' I just wanted to have fun and we had nothing better to do.

Because I had never really appreciated that I was ill, I found it impossible to behave as my parents would wish. That's just how I was. My condition was probably less at the forefront of my mind than it was for Mum. They called it being ill; I called it being me. Of course, I knew I had a delicate stomach because Mum and Dad were always trying to protect it. But it wasn't in my thoughts every minute of every day. It's still not.

So there I was at the top of the stairs with Hannah, and I remember thinking, 'I'll be fine.'

How wrong I was.

The slide down was exhilarating but brief. At the end of it, I stood up, and that's when Hannah screamed. I looked down. My stoma had ruptured. It wasn't part of me, so I didn't feel anything – it didn't hurt at all. But it made a huge mess.

Mum appeared and started shouting at me. She didn't have a clue at that stage what had happened, and she must have feared the worst. But she could see I wasn't in pain. If anything I think I was in shock. The sight of so much blood made me feel sick.

But not as sick as Hannah.

In the end, Dad had to drive her home. 'She'll be traumatised for a good while yet,' he lectured me. 'I hope you've learned your lesson.'

Dad wanted to take me to the hospital in case I'd done serious damage to the stoma but that was the last place I wanted to go. Once we had checked that I could still catheterise and I'd promised not to be so stupid again he said I could stay at home – but if there were any signs of problems I'd be marched straight back to Yorkhill.

On another occasion, when I was about six, I really did hurt myself – but once again it was a friend who bore the brunt of it.

Kenneth used to play the bagpipes, and when he wasn't using them they were stored in his room in the big case they came in. The case was huge, with sharp corners to protect it. He was practising one afternoon when his friend, Greg, came round to see him. Mum and Dad had drilled into him that he had to put the pipes away if he wasn't using them, so he did. But he left the case in the hallway.

On my way into the lounge, I collided with Greg, who was walking out and accidentally knocked me into the case. I felt my breath disappear as my feet vanished from under me. I didn't have a chance to move and landed with my stomach right on the sharp edge.

It all happened so quickly, and it took me quite a few seconds to realise how much agony I was in. And then I started to scream.

I've never seen Dad so angry. He was raging at poor Greg for being so stupid. He was only worried about me, but Greg feared for his life, I think. He fled the house and ran up the street.

I didn't blame Greg, but that didn't make my pain go away. I was doubled over. My stomach was so sore I thought I was going to be sick, although I managed to hold it back. It didn't bleed but the pain more than made up for how innocuous it looked.

I sat on the floor holding my stomach, sobbing. Mum and Dad started fussing over me, anxious to find out what damage there was.

'You'll have to drain,' Mum said.

'It's not time,' I replied.

'Tough. We've got to check if you're OK.'

I hated being drained at the best of times. Sometimes there was a burning sensation that I couldn't get rid of. Other times my skin just felt raw where the catheter had to slide into me. This occasion was even worse.

I was screaming, 'Get off me! Leave me alone!'

I really fought them that time, but Mum won in the end. Throughout the whole ordeal all I could hear was Dad saying, 'Are you OK? Are you OK?'

And I remember thinking, 'of course I'm not OK.' All I could think about was how much I was suffering there and then. Mum and Dad were more concerned about the long-term effects. I was already in so much discomfort with the leaking from my stoma. Had I made it worse? I never really thought about that but I suppose my parents never stopped worrying.

MARTIN: One of the most refreshing things about Kirsteen as she's got older has been the way she just deals with life.

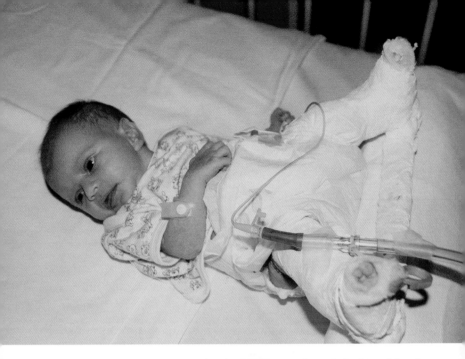

Above Only days old and in ward 2b at Yorkhill. My legs are in plaster and my feet are wedged apart to allow the initial repairs to heal.

Left Enjoying the swing at the Sea Life Centre in Oban, 1995. Despite my medical troubles, I was always ready to have fun!

Left Playing with my big brothers Kenneth and Martin Jr in 1995.

Below Some of the worst times at Great Ormond Street Hospital (GOSH) following major surgical procedures in September and October 2000.

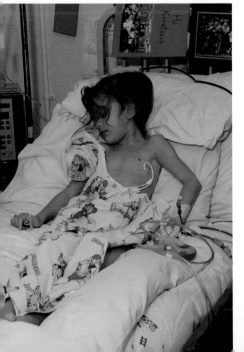

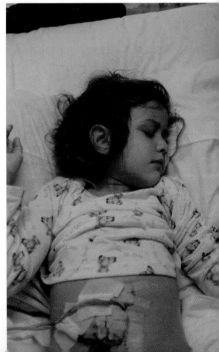

Above Well on the mend now! Mr Philip Ransley (superhero!!!) pointing to his handiwork in March 2001 at GOSH.

Below My favourite nurse Marika Clow, now a great family friend who sadly (for us) now lives in Australia!

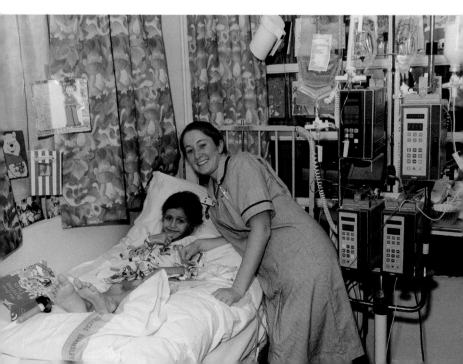

Left On a bike ride (wearing our GOSH clothes) with my big brothers and dad.

Below With HRH Sophie, Countess of Wessex, in the official line-up for the GOSH carol service at St Paul's Kensington in 2004. I was introduced by Sir Trevor McDonald.

Above This is me as Mr Smee in Craigdhu Primary School's Christmas Pantomime 2004.

Right Mr Jason Isaacs, who is a great supporter of GOSH, at the launch of *Peter Pan in Scarlet* at Kensington Palace in October 2006. Jason (who plays the evil Lucius Malfoy in the *Harry Potter* films) gave us a personally guided tour of the set of the most recent movie the following week … top man indeed!

Left With John Nettles at the Jersey Crystal Ball in September 2005, an event at which I spoke about my experiences at GOSH.

Right With Carol Vorderman at a special dinner held on the night before the 'Pride of Britain' awards ceremony.

Left Jude Law presented me with my 'Pride of Britain' award. Here we are at the after-show party.

Below With Gary Lineker and Dame Kelly Holmes at the after-show party for the 'Pride of Britain' awards.

Above I also got to meet Mr (anything but nasty!) Simon Cowell at the after-show party.

Below All the 'Pride of Britain' winners visited Number 10 the morning after the event – it was amazing to get to see inside the home of the PM!

We thought she would have been a shrinking violet and suffer at the hands of her contemporaries. But she's always been a fighter – literally where her brother Martin is concerned. There's a crack in his bedroom door where she kicked it, trying to chase him a few years ago. But when she was younger, we had the very real dilemma of trying to balance giving her freedom with protecting her as much as we could from other people. We never wanted her to feel ashamed or embarrassed about her condition, but on the other hand we never wanted to make her a target for cruel words.

All these fears came to a head as soon as she was signed up for nursery and pre-school. Jill's always been an upfront person, and from the day that Kirsteen was born we've told everyone about her condition. We didn't want anyone gossiping or whispering behind her back asking, 'What's wrong with her? I've heard she's got three heads.' We wanted to leave no room for conjecture as to what she had. We thought the best policy was to be open about it.

So while we didn't quite make an announcement when she joined nursery, we made sure the teachers knew and that any parents Jill spoke to were put in the picture as well. A lot of the families were local and knew all about Kirsteen anyway, so there wasn't really much of a story, but it was best to get it clear from the start. Then, when Kirsteen started pre-school, it was the same. All the parents and staff were in the loop. By the time she began at primary school we were quite used to the process of informing everyone.

But that was also when we really started to worry.

There were three things that concerned us. The first was the fact that Kirsteen was extremely delicate around her abdomen area. It was a daily fear of mine that she would be injured in some run-of-the-mill high jinks.

'What if she falls off her chair?' I asked Jill. 'What if she slips on the reading rug?'

Jill had the same fears as me but she kept them in check. 'What if, what if, what if? There's nothing we can do.'

The school assigned a special needs teacher – Mrs Dot Clark, who is still a friend – to Kirsteen while she was there, which eased our concerns to some extent. Mrs Clark knew Kirsteen from nursery, so there was already a bond there. But the knowledge that neither Jill nor I was watching her took some getting used to. The phrase 'out of sight, out of mind' really didn't work in this instance.

Then there was the fact that she was still wearing nappies at the age of five. Jill and I projected all sorts of fears about how this could affect her development. What if she felt like a baby? It could hold her back emotionally for years. You can tell all the parents and teachers you like, but kids are another proposition. They can be so cruel. If Kirsteen's classmates discovered she was different like that her life could be ruined.

The biggest threat to Kirsteen's happiness was her need to drain. Despite so many months of doing it, the process continued to cause her a lot of discomfort. Trying to find the hole where the catheter was inserted was still very much trial and error. It didn't help that she tensed her body because she was expecting the sore jab of pain. The only thing in our favour was the fact that by the time she started school the regularity with which she needed to catheterise had reduced to once every three or four hours. Mrs Clark could drain her if necessary, but although Kirsteen didn't mind – she was almost like a member of the family – I don't think Dot was comfortable doing it. Fortunately, we worked out that if she drained just before school, she could last until lunchtime. So every day Jill walked to the school to pick her up and dropped her off again in the afternoon.

One of the things Kirsteen still couldn't do was swim. Both our boys were introduced to water early on. But with the nappy needing to be worn at all times because of her leaking, the presence of her stoma and the essential need to keep the area spotlessly clean, this was a no-go area for Kirsteen. If her classmates all went to the pool, she had to stand at the side or wait with the special needs teacher. Our plan for her to not feel 'different' or excluded had its limitations. We just hoped they wouldn't overly damage her confidence.

PE in general was another problem. Young kids in school have to get changed together in the classroom. It's been like that since I was a boy, although I don't know why. Shortly after she started primary school Kirsteen told me, 'I think it's ridiculous making boys and girls get changed in front of everyone.' She was usually allowed to get changed in the toilets (we'd made it clear to the teaching staff that Kirsteen would need a bit of privacy whenever she took her clothes off), so she wasn't even arguing the cause for herself; I think it was a problem for some of her friends who felt a little self-conscious with the boys.

But on one occasion, Kirsteen was not given the opportunity to change on her own, and that opened a whole can of worms.

It was Christmas, and Kirsteen's class was taking part in the festive play. Mrs Clark was wonderful; she always looked after her really well, ensuring she had the privacy she needed. But this time, with a speedy costume change required, she didn't.

'Aren't we going out to the toilets?' Kirsteen asked.

'We haven't got time,' she was told.

'But what if someone sees me?'

'Nobody's watching you. Come on, quickly now.'

But somebody was watching. A little boy happened to be looking over. He told one of the girls. Together, the pair watched as Mrs Clark helped Kirsteen out of her clothes – and they both saw the obvious fact that Kirsteen was wearing a nappy.

'Miss! Miss!' the boy called out. 'Why is Kirsteen wearing a nappy?'

Immediately, thirty pairs of eyes were on Kirsteen.

'Oh no!' she cried and pulled her costume over her as quickly as possible. But it was too late. They'd all seen what she was wearing – and they knew it had nothing to do with the play they were about to perform.

The teachers responded very well. They tried to deflect attention and instructed the children to hurry up. But the buzz continued, and the fact that Kirsteen had erupted into tears confirmed that they were right.

'Baby! Baby!' one boy shouted.

'Where's your dummy?' called another.

A lot of the children in her class had known Kirsteen since she was born and they simply accepted her. They weren't the ones trying to humiliate her. It was the boys and girls from other areas who were being so cruel.

Kirsteen was too upset to continue in the play, so she sat with Mrs Clark in the classroom until it was time to go home.

'What's wrong?' I asked Jill as she brought Kirsteen through the front door, her face red and puffy from crying.

Kirsteen could barely explain through her tears and I could only make out the occasional phrase.

'I'm never going back there! I hate it! Take me out of school! I hate it! I never want to go there again!'

Getting her to go back the next day was a trial, involving a combination of bribes, mild threats and downright lies. Mrs Clark met her personally at the school gates and escorted her in. She couldn't apologise enough for causing the problem, but assured us she was working with the class teacher to resolve it.

The next few weeks were touch and go. One afternoon Kirsteen would be fine, the next she'd be flinging herself onto her bed distraught again. It only needed one person to mention something for her to be thrown straight back into despair.

All her life she had thought everybody accepted her for what she was. Even her grandmother's poisonous views had been kept from her up until now. Now, for the first time, she realised that other people thought she was different.

'Why can't I be normal?' she cried one day. 'Why am I the only one who has to wear this?'

I wished we could have answered her. It was a harrowing period, and my heart broke watching her go through it. Jill and I had been waiting for a disaster like this. All those nights when the kids were in bed and we sat talking, worrying what her life was going to be like, fretting if she was ever going to have anything like a normal life, came back to me. This was our nightmare come true.

I suppose we should have been grateful that this was the only time she'd really been made to feel an outcast. But who knew how long it would go on for? The sooner we could be seen by Great Ormond Street the better.

Knowing that our appointment in London was coming up was the only thing that calmed Kirsteen. When the day arrived, she could hardly contain herself. Jill and I felt the same as we made the journey down to London the night before. By the time morning came, we were all beside ourselves with anticipation. Would this be the end of all the problems? Or could we be told how far away the end was?

Stepping through the doors in Great Ormond Street immediately brought back the feelings of security, trust and belief that we'd left with last time. Our meeting was with the consultant Philip Ransley – the man who had spoken to the BEES group meeting on our last visit. He would be conducting the exploratory operation on Kirsteen under anaesthetic to assess what could be done for her.

I was relieved to discover that Mr Ransley was as personable on a one-to-one basis as he was when addressing a packed conference room. He was a very distinguished, dapper-looking chap, very laid-back, with quite a droll character and a good sense of humour. What really mattered though, was that he had a friendly face and immediately put Kirsteen at ease. He treated her like an adult and spoke directly to her as much as to us. We felt instantly that we were in safe hands.

KIRSTEEN: My earliest memory of Great Ormond Street is the visit when I had to have an operation so that Mr Ransley could look at me and see what state I was in. From the moment I woke up in our hotel that morning I remember Mum buzzing around nervously.

The night before she had told me that I might not have to have another operation if this one went well, so that morning I had mixed feelings. I was half wishing and half cursing. Part of me was thinking, 'I'd better not have to have another one', while another part thought, 'At least the end is in sight.' A third part was just really upset that I'd have to go through another procedure at all – even if it was to be the last.

I'll never forget walking through the doors of Great Ormond Street for the first time. I had just turned six years old, and it's as clear in my memory as if it were yesterday.

Usually you go into a hospital and you see people looking sad in the visitors' area; you hear kids crying because they're getting jabs or recovering from an operation; and you see the staff wandering around looking busy and not that interested in smiling. At Great Ormond Street even the parents look cheerful. They know how ill their children are, but they do their best to look happy so that their child can be happy as well. The whole hospital seems geared towards making this happen. I think that's really nice.

The atmosphere is the same throughout all the wards. Whenever I entered Yorkhill, it seemed to me to be quite a scary place, and I was always struck by the sense that there is illness everywhere, and that people are probably dying there. That's all you can think of. But at Great Ormond Street they make such an effort to lift people's spirits. They distract the patients and their visitors with plenty of toys and activities, like clowns and entertainers. Everywhere you look you see lots of kids playing. You see how ill everyone is and wonder how that works. How do they manage to make it seem so pleasant?

It's a very colourful place, not like a normal depressing, grey hospital. But it's not just the brightness that makes it stand out. One of the main differences is that there's no smell. I don't know how they do it because every other hospital smells of Dettol or some other cleaning product. The smell normally hits you as soon as you step through the door. Great Ormond Street is spotlessly clean but it smells of comforting things, not disinfectant. There's a really friendly environment. I think it's as nice as a hospital can get.

It's impossible not to think positively from the moment you walk in. I noticed it as soon as I stepped into one of the wards and thought, 'If I have to spend another minute in a hospital, I want it to be this one.'

Really, though, I didn't want to spend another second in any hospital. Not as a patient. But before the day was out I would be undergoing another general anaesthetic and having my insides explored and probed. And as nice and comforting as I found the place, I really wasn't looking forward to it.

When I came round from the surgery, Mum and Dad were, as usual, at my bedside. It feels like waking up after a really long sleep but it takes ages for your head to clear. Normally, I look around the room and try to focus on the scenery. Sometimes I struggle to remember where I am. All I really know is, it doesn't get any easier – or more pleasant – with practice.

As soon as I was fully conscious, Mr Ransley told us what he'd discovered. I felt so lethargic, but I knew that what he said next could shape the rest of my life. As far as I knew, he had fixed any problems already. But there was also a chance he'd learned I was beyond help. Looking at his body language, I couldn't honestly guess at what he was going to say.

'Well, I've had a good root round,' he explained. 'What's been done so far looks reasonably OK.

He also said that he didn't think there would be a problem closing up the urethra. It was a long time since he'd seen a stoma but he was sure he could conceal it to the extent that just a little flap of skin would be on the surface.

I could see Mum and Dad were really happy with that news. I suppose I was as well. I couldn't get too excited though. I'd been given good news before – and had been let down.

Also, it meant I was due to have at least one more operation. 'Is it never going to end?' I thought. 'I don't know if I can take any more of this.'

I knew I had to be positive though. I've never been one to mope around. I get upset sometimes, but only if someone says something to me that I find hurtful. I don't like feeling sorry for myself, not like some people who like to moan if they have the slightest threat of a toothache or a sore toe.

Once I'd stopped feeling so emotional, I realised Mr Ransley was being serious. 'I think if you come here as an inpatient we'll be able to put you right in a few hours,' he told me.

These were the words I'd been waiting to hear all my life. But there was a snag.

Looking at my parents, he said, 'As you probably know, I'm afraid we have a waiting list here. It's going to be a year before I can get to see Kirsteen again.'

My heart sank. Another year of wearing nappies. Another year of pain when I had to catheterise.

Another year of being 'different'.

CHAPTER 10
Tell Daddy I Love Him

KIRSTEEN: I do have many happy memories from Great Ormond Street, but one of my earliest is less happy. I remember sitting in a room crying. When you're six years old, being told that you have to wait another year for anything seems like a lifetime. But when you're waiting for an operation that could change your life, it's unbearable. Even after the operation I knew that I would still have to catheterise for the rest of my life – but at least I would be out of nappies. My stoma wouldn't leak, I wouldn't hurt – and I wouldn't be a laughing stock at school.

'They're never going to fix me,' I sobbed.

'Of course they are,' Mum said. 'Mr Ransley's just very busy at the minute. He's got lots of other little boys and girls to see to first.'

Realising that I wasn't alone with my condition actually helped me. Since our holiday in Mull when I was young,

Jane Wallace had stayed in touch with Mum and Dad – and their daughter Inya had become a really good friend of mine. Even though she was ten years older, we have this thing in common which nobody else can really relate to. She'd called me just before I went down to Great Ormond Street to wish me good luck, which I really appreciated.

While I was down in London I got the opportunity to help someone else.

Mum and Dad knew lots of people through the BEES support network. Our visit to London coincided with another family's operation date. Their little girl was younger than I was, and at first I was jealous that she was being seen to so much earlier than me, but I soon pushed that out of my head.

'Their little girl's very scared,' Mum said. 'She doesn't like the idea of being operated on.'

'Maybe I should talk to her?' I suggested.

'I think she'd really like that.'

As soon as I was able to walk after Mr Ransley's exploratory op, we all went to the Louise Ward where my parents' friends were with their daughter. When we arrived, the girl was reading a book with pink fairy stickers in it. She was smaller than me and she looked so frightened. I told her there was nothing to worry about.

'I've had eight operations,' I said. 'You don't even know they're happening, and then you wake up and it's all over.'

The little girl couldn't believe I'd had so many.

'Will I have to have eight operations?' she asked.

I explained that I had been unlucky. 'I think you'll only need one,' I said. 'And this time next year I'm going to have the same one.'

Before we left, I asked where her book had come from

and she told me she thought her mum had bought it in the hospital shop.

It was time for us to leave. We went back down to our room to collect our things, and, as soon as we were on our own again, I became upset. Why didn't we come here when I was small? I wondered. I know my parents were thinking the same thing. I was still miserable when we left the hospital, but just before we stepped outside Mum said, 'Your dad's got something for you.'

I don't know how he managed it without me noticing, but in his hands was a copy of the pink fairy book. I left Great Ormond Street with a great big smile on my face. And I couldn't wait to come back.

MARTIN: I know all about hospital waiting lists so it was no surprise to me when we were told we would have to come back in almost a year's time. Knowing didn't make the waiting any easier, though. Having said that, when Kirsteen was being treated at Yorkhill we'd never really had a sense of where each operation stood in relation to her overall long-term health. Now, as hard as it was waiting for so long to go back to London, at least we knew it was the final hurdle. In a few months' time it would all be behind us.

JILL: Or at least that's what we thought.

MARTIN: In September 2000, just a few weeks before her seventh birthday, Kirsteen was admitted into Great Ormond Street. The waiting was over.

The timing was very awkward for us. A few weeks earlier and it would have fallen nicely into the summer holidays. As it was we had to bring the boys out of school for a few days at the start of the academic year. It went totally against our principles to make them suffer because of Kirsteen – although in this instance they weren't complaining – but even though it was an important time for them in their new classes, we couldn't see any other way.

We all caught the train down and tried to pretend we were going on a little holiday. It was Kenneth and Martin's first time in London so they were excited, although I don't think they enjoyed the long journey. I'd promised to take them to see Buckingham Palace and a few of the other sights, so they were looking forward to that. Kirsteen joined in the fun as well, but I knew she was nervous about what was coming up. Normally, we didn't tell her about operations until the day before, but this one had been on the calendar for so long that she'd had plenty of time to adjust to it. That didn't mean she wasn't scared, though.

And Jill and I couldn't let on that we were too.

One of the many incredible things about Great Ormond Street is the way it looks after the families of its patients. Because all its patients are children, it also has to be equipped to meet their parents' needs. I have to say it does this remarkably well. Mums and dads are not made to feel in the way on the wards as they can at other hospitals. The policy appears to be that anything that makes the child feel better is OK. And in most cases having mothers and fathers around does just that.

But that costs money. Just staying in London can be a financial drain for a lot of people, and I have to admit that Jill and I were no different. The expense of going to London was certainly a concern when the idea was first mentioned to us by BEES. But Great Ormond Street, I was amazed to learn, had that area covered too.

Because the hospital takes cases from all over the UK it is cognisant of the fact that not everyone can afford to stay in hotels in London to be near their children, and that no child's health should be put at risk because of this. So for parents like us, there is free accommodation available in nearby Trust house buildings owned by the hospital. You have a private bedroom and share a communal lounge, bathroom and kitchen. It's not the Ritz – but it felt like it to us. For a lot of families it could be the difference between getting their child the best medical help in the world – or not.

I don't know how, but we would have found the money somehow if necessary. Fortunately, however, that was one pressure Great Ormond Street relieved us of months in advance. And, as Jill and I settled into our family room, we felt a great sense of well-being because of it.

'We're so close now,' I said. 'I've got a good feeling about this.'

Kirsteen was officially admitted by the hospital that afternoon and we helped her to settle into the Louise Ward with the other urology patients. There were lots of paintings and drawings on the walls, obviously made by other children, which was very welcoming. A great effort had gone into making the place as unintimidating as possible.

Another facility that Great Ormond Street offers is a day school for brothers and sisters of patients, but neither Kenneth nor Martin seemed too keen on this. They were more interested in the PlayStation next to Kirsteen's bed. All the children in there had these, and little televisions as well. The atmosphere really was extraordinarily light considering the work that goes on in that ward.

The nurses were extremely nice and did their best to make us feel as comfortable as possible ahead of the following morning's operation. Even so, all our nerves were on edge because we knew how important the next few days would be for Kirsteen.

As six o'clock came and went I said to Jill, 'We'd better be getting these boys fed and into bed.'

She took one look at Kirsteen and said, 'I'm going to stay here.'

'I don't think you'll be allowed,' I said. But once again I had underestimated Great Ormond Street.

'I'm afraid we don't have a spare bed but you're welcome to stay in that chair,' the ward sister told Jill.

The next morning Jill and I were taken aside by the senior registrar, Mr Imran Mushtaq (now a consultant at the hospital). I was expecting him to tell us that today's operation would be the medical equivalent of crossing a few Ts and dotting Is, but that wasn't the case.

'I know that Mr Ransley told you that what we are doing today is straightforward, and it is,' he said. 'But you need to know that it is actually an enormous procedure.'

A sickening feeling came over me. I had taken 'straightforward' to mean a bit of tidying up. I hadn't appreciated the severity of what was required.

As Mr Mushtaq left us, I felt the blood drain from my head. Dozens of thoughts were colliding with each other and I struggled to make sense of what we had been told.

'Are they starting from the beginning again?' I asked Jill. 'What if they have the same problems the other doctors had?'

But one question in particular seemed to stick in my throat. Had everything we had put Kirsteen through over the last six years been for nothing? The idea that we were in some way responsible for any unnecessary suffering was impossible to bear.

But it was important that Jill and I didn't show our concern to Kirsteen. Once more, we went through the familiar pattern of watching her being wheeled down to theatre. Once more, I felt sick with fear as the anaesthetic was administered. And, once more, I thought, all we can do now is wait.

I don't know if it was for my own benefit or theirs, but while the operation was taking place I took the boys out for some fresh air. There are lots of cafés and parks near the hospital and it's the sort of area where you can easily lose an afternoon before you know it. Not on this occasion, though. As the boys ran around and let off steam, I couldn't help checking my watch every five minutes. Time seemed to be passing so slowly I thought my watch might have broken.

By the time we got back to the hospital Jill was all smiles. 'Mr Ransley's very happy,' she told me. 'He says it all went to plan. They've made Kirsteen's bladder bigger and closed her urethra. And they said she'll be able to go home in about ten days.'

I breathed a sigh of relief as I watched Kirsteen sleep in a little curtained-off area of the ward. She was attached to a drip as usual, but I was used to this by now. She also had an external stent catheter strapped to her. A stent is a wire mesh tube that keeps an incision open while the catheter is plugged in. It looked a little unpleasant, but I was told that it was just there to drain the urine until the operation had settled. 'Perfectly standard procedure.'

It was as though an enormous weight had been lifted from my shoulders. And the good news continued a few days later.

One of the reasons I hadn't been too keen to disrupt the boys' lives by bringing them down to London was because of Kenneth's birthday. As it turned out, we were in Great Ormond Street the day he turned ten. The nurses all made a fuss of him but that wasn't all. 'We've got some special guests coming later,' one of them told him.

That afternoon, as a special treat for the patients, some pilots from the famous Red Arrows flying team stopped by to talk about their work and show the children pictures of their aeroplanes. Both the boys were incredibly excited as soon as the men walked through the door. And when the pilots learned that it was Kenneth's birthday, they singled him out for special treatment and even sang 'Happy Birthday' to him.

KENNETH: It was wonderful experience and it came completely out of the blue, but I remember feeling really guilty. The Red Arrows pilots made a real fuss of me, asking me all about what I was up to, what my hobbies were and where I lived, but I just thought, 'There are all these sick people around here and I'm hogging all the attention.' I was a bit uneasy about that, and it was a little embarrassing when they got everyone to sing to me, but I was in my element when they started talking about their planes and all the stunts they did. I was really into aeroplanes and the Red Arrows and all that kind of stuff so it was a dream come true just to meet them. When they asked me what my name was I thought I was going to burst with pride.

I never really got to know Yorkhill because I was too young, so all my impressions of hospitals are based on Great Ormond Street. It's a wonderful place. They spend so much time there trying to find new ways to help the patients recover more quickly.

There's even a 'play leader' on every ward whose job it is to look after the brothers and sisters of the patients, and try to make sure they have as good a time as possible in the hospital. It sounds a bit excessive, but I know from my own experience that anything you can do to distract kids is a good thing.

Because I was young, I couldn't fully understand what was going on in Great Ormond Street. I knew Kirsteen was ill and that they were going to make her better, but I didn't know the ins and outs of it all, or how serious things were. Looking back, I think it was a good thing Martin and I were too young to appreciate just how ill our sister was. If she was in that situation now I don't think I could cope with it. I don't know if I'd have the strength.

It makes perfect sense to keep the truth from children – Mum and Dad had enough to deal with without Martin and me being upset too. And that's where the play leaders and all the nurses were so brilliant. I remember once sitting in Kirsteen's room reading the latest Harry Potter book. I was aware that there was a lot of activity around me because the doctors were trying to do some tests, and I pretty much ignored it, being used to that sort of thing. But suddenly Kirsteen started screaming blue murder and I realised something was wrong. That was the first time it really shook me. I wanted the doctors to stop hurting her but I knew they were just trying to help. That was a defining moment, I think, for me.

Then the door was flung open and the play leader appeared and dragged Martin and me away. In retrospect, I think that was pretty amazing. Just when you thought everyone's attention would be on helping Kirsteen, they found time to make sure we weren't too traumatised.

MARTIN: It meant so much to Jill and me that Kenneth and Martin could have fun. It was bad enough them being dragged around Glasgow while we looked after Kirsteen, but pulling them out of school and away from their friends to go to London was even worse. Jill and I decided that as soon as Kirsteen was close to being herself again, I would take the boys back home. The girls could return whenever Kirsteen was signed out.

So that's what we did.

'Love you, Kirsteen,' I said, cuddling her as we said goodbye. 'You get your strength back and I'll see you at home before you know it.'

The train journey from London's Euston to Glasgow Central takes about five and a half hours, and that return trip seemed to fly by. The boys were excited about seeing their friends again and I was planning the rest of my week.

What really lightened the mood, of course, was knowing that Kirsteen was on the final straight of her journey to recovery. The next time I see her, I thought, in just over a week, she'll be home, ready to start the rest of her life.

JILL: Martin had only been gone a few hours when it became obvious there was a problem. Something was wrong with the contents of the urine collection bag that was attached to Kirsteen. It filled up gradually throughout the day and a nurse would check the full bag every time she replaced it with a fresh one. On the first day there had been no problem. By the second day I wasn't even taking any notice of it any more and I don't think Kirsteen was either.

But on this occasion something about the nurse's manner seemed unusual.

'That's odd,' she said, examining the bag.

'What's wrong?' I asked, but I could see the drainage bag looked green in the light.

'I'm not sure but it looks like something is getting into Kirsteen's urine,' she said. 'At a guess I would say it was faecal matter. But the doctor can tell us more.'

I wished I hadn't asked in front of Kirsteen. It was too late though. I could see she had heard every word.

But that, as it turned out, was the least of my worries.

They decided to connect Kirsteen to a regular drip – a procedure she'd undergone dozens of times before. It was uncomfortable having a tube attached to her hand, but at least she knew it helped.

A nurse arrived to connect the drip but she couldn't find a suitable vein through which to insert the needle. She tried again. And again.

I watched open-mouthed while this was going on. I'd seen it done so many times before, and I couldn't understand. 'What's the problem?' I asked.

'I can't find a vein.'

Another nurse and a doctor came over. They each tried repeatedly to find a vein, without success. They were trying to remain calm but suddenly there was terrible panic in the room. I could see it in the staff's eyes. They didn't know what to do. Whatever was wrong with Kirsteen's urine bag had affected her whole body.

One of the nurses grabbed the ward telephone and within minutes an anaesthetist came running in.

He took one look at Kirsteen and said, 'I'll give it one shot. If it doesn't work, she's going into theatre. We've got no choice.'

I could barely breathe as I watched the anaesthetist. Kirsteen was crying and her little hand felt so small and limp in mine, but I had to keep squeezing it, reassuring her that everything was going to be fine.

I just wished I believed it myself.

The anaesthetist was running his hands all over Kirsteen's arms and legs, looking for a vein that hadn't been damaged. 'Time's running out,' I thought. I could barely bring myself to watch.

Kirsteen was beginning to struggle for breath. Another trolley was brought over with a large canister of oxygen and a mask. While the anaesthetist continued his work a nurse reached over and clasped the mask over Kirsteen's mouth.

Instinctively, she tried to rip it off. I did my best to calm her but she was beginning to get hysterical. 'I'm going to die,' she cried. 'I'm going to die.'

I'd never seen her so scared. 'Don't be silly, Kirsteen, you're going to be fine, you're going to be fine.' I kept repeating it. But I looked at the nurses and they were in tears; they knew how bad she was.

I watched as the anaesthetist picked up Kirsteen's foot.

'Got it!' he said.

A huge collective sigh went round the room. He'd managed to get the needle into a vein in Kirsteen's heel. After fifteen attempts he'd found the only place that hadn't stopped working.

My hand felt all clammy in Kirsteen's. 'You're going to be all right,' I kept whispering, but I don't even know if she could hear me through her sobs.

I wished that Martin was there, and telephoned him as soon as I could. I explained what was going on. 'She looks so poorly,' I said.

He and the boys had only been home an hour but there was only one thing on his mind.

'I'll see for myself tomorrow,' he said. 'We'll get the first train down.'

I knew it was a great upheaval for Martin with his work and the boys' schooling, but I was so relieved to hear his words.

Over the next few hours several doctors put their heads together. Then Mr Ransley took me aside and confided they didn't know what was happening.

'I've never seen this before,' he said, 'although I heard about a similar case about twenty years ago. I can't honestly tell you what is going wrong but I can tell you what it might be.'

The most likely explanation, he said, was that a little hole called a fistula had opened up and a connection had been made between the bowel and bladder. 'The procedure went as planned,' he confirmed. 'If I'm right about this then it should remedy itself within a week or so.'

Even though, on the one hand, I was getting myself worked up that something was seriously wrong and that Mr Ransley didn't know what it was, on the other hand I found it very refreshing that he had been so honest and upfront with me. It takes a big man, particularly one in his position, to admit when they don't know something.

But the thought of just sitting there with our fingers crossed and doing nothing terrified me.

And what Mr Ransley told me next made me feel even worse.

In order to give the bowel and bladder a chance to heal he had to ensure they weren't used. And that meant 'nil by mouth' for Kirsteen. No food, no fluid, no feeding at all.

Just when we thought things were turning around she was hit with this.

He explained that they would operate to insert something called a Hickman line into Kirsteen to provide nourishment – a relatively routine procedure, we were told, but, as usual, anything requiring anaesthetic scared me. The doctors would make a little nick in a vein in her neck and then insert a tube – the Hickman line – down into the heart. A drip bag would then be hooked on a frame over her.

Martin and the boys arrived the next morning. There was only so much I could say in front of Kenneth and wee Martin but I was just so glad to see them. I'd lost count of how many operations Kirsteen had had in her short life, but all I knew was that I don't think I could have coped if I'd had to endure this one alone. The night before had been bad enough – us stuck in London while Martin was hundreds of miles away; all Kirsteen could say was, 'I want Daddy.'

'He'll be here by the time you wake up,' I'd promised. And thank God he was.

Not long after they arrived, Kirsteen was taken down to theatre again. When she came back from the operation, I noticed that her drip looked different from usual. Normally they contain saline or some clear-looking liquid, but the contents of this one looked like powdered milk and, I was told, contained all the nutrition Kirsteen needed.

Just as well, I thought as I looked at her. That's all she'll be getting for the next couple of weeks.

Later that night Mr Ransley told me he was leaving for a lecture tour of Italy. By the time he returned he expected to find Kirsteen well on the mend. I prayed he was right.

Over the next week we got into a nice routine. I spent every minute I could by Kirsteen's bedside. She seemed to be getting thinner by the hour but I couldn't show I was worried. Putting on as brave a face as I could, I made a point of befriending a few of the nurses and Kirsteen and I got chatting to them every time they came by. They were all lovely, but a couple of them, Evelyn and Marika, took a particular shine to Kirsteen and she really responded to them. They did their very best to take her mind off things.

Martin stayed down for three days. We were told that the Hickman line should tidy everything up within a fortnight, and he wanted to make sure it was doing its job before he left again. But being in London was tough on the boys. So, in the morning he'd pop in to see Kirsteen for a while, giving me a chance to spend time with Kenneth and Martin. Then we'd swap over again and he'd take the lads out for the afternoon. Over the next few days they visited the Natural History Museum, the RAF Museum, the Science Museum and they even did an open-top bus tour around all the tourist spots. They had fun; I only wish they didn't have to experience the downside as well.

MARTIN JR: It was great being taken all over London. I felt really sorry for Kirsteen because she was missing out, but we always made a point of picking up souvenirs or programmes for her to see when we got back. I don't know if it meant much to her but we wanted to show her we were thinking about her.

Mum and Dad tried hard to make sure we weren't upset or bored, but it wasn't always possible. All those dead long journeys up to Great Ormond Street and back really stay in my memory. The first few times I thought they were never going to end. But I remember walking into the hospital for the first time and seeing this big red London bus by the entrance. That was always there. Whenever I saw that I smiled. I knew we had arrived then.

Even though Dad did his best to fill our days, there was one thing he couldn't do anything about. We were so young that we got tired quite easily. After a day out at a museum Dad couldn't wait to go and see Kirsteen. I remember night after night at the hospital, being so tired that I couldn't keep my eyes open, but Dad couldn't bear to leave Kirsteen to take us back to the Trust house until visiting was over. At home I always thought it was really cool to stay up later than my bed time, but when it actually happened I struggled. I couldn't wait to get back to my own house and my own bed. I just wished Mum and Kirsteen could come with us.

JILL: One night during her stay in the hospital, Kirsteen and I got chatting to a couple of the other patients. A darling little seven-year-old boy called Alex was put into the bed next to Kirsteen's. He had had a cancerous tumour on his kidney but was now, they thought, getting better. Even though the two children had very different problems, they got on instantly, and his parents were really nice as well. It was heart-warming to watch the kids chat to each other as if they didn't have a care in the world.

But we were soon reminded of the truth. It seemed to come out of the blue. One minute Kirsteen was coping with her 'nil-by-mouth' diet as well as could be expected, the next she'd started to go downhill. She was shedding weight too quickly and her strength had all but disappeared.

I was shocked at how quickly the transformation had happened.

Yet again, there was a flurry of white coats around her bed. One of the doctors soon grasped that the Hickman line had become infected, which meant it could no longer be used. No one had expected this – and Mr Ransley still wasn't due back.

Kirsteen's temperature was spiking to extreme levels, and the big problem now was that they could not administer any liquid or food by any other means. Without drastic action, she was unlikely to last the week.

A urology consultant who was deputising for Mr Ransley warned that he might be forced to perform a temporary colostomy operation on Kirsteen. This was very much a last resort – it would involve bypassing her bowel – but would at least mean that she could start consuming food by mouth again.

The doctors all knew that Kirsteen was really too ill for this operation, but they were rapidly running out of options. Before any decision was made, the consultant requested new scans. But she was too ill even to be taken to the scanning room.

It was Kirsteen herself who came up with the solution to this problem, though. 'Don't move me,' she begged. 'Bring the equipment here.'

I thought she was delirious. But the doctors listened to her and all the machinery and computers they needed were brought up to the ward. Kirsteen became upset again. She was drifting in and out of consciousness. I don't think she knew what she was saying – but that didn't stop her words breaking my heart.

'I'm going to die and I'm scared,' she cried. 'But tell Daddy I love him and I'll miss him.'

What do you say to that? I said what I always said. 'Oh, Kirsteen, don't you worry. You'll be fine. Everything's all right. You're in safe hands now.'

But as soon as the doctors started the scans I ran out of the ward to the public telephone. I just prayed Martin was at home.

I was in luck.

'Martin,' I said. 'She's really bad. I don't care how you do it, I don't care what it costs, but I want you down here tomorrow morning.'

MARTIN: That was the worst day of my life. Without exception I have never felt as bad as I did when I took that call.

I'll never forget the moment the phone rang. I was in the middle of tiling the bathroom floor to take my mind off what was going on in London. Any other time, I would have let it ring off and hope the caller left a message. But I couldn't afford to ignore any calls these days.

I shudder to think what would have happened had I not picked up.

Jill was distraught. Through all that had happened where Kirsteen was concerned, this was my darkest hour.

Imagine being told your daughter thinks she's going to die – she's in a hospital bed in London crying out your name – and you're stuck, helpless, 400 miles away in Glasgow.

I couldn't get a train reservation fast enough. I didn't want to panic the boys, but I was pulling my hair out. I didn't know how I was going to hold it together.

By coincidence, there was a knock at the door a few minutes later. It was our neighbour, Usha Marwaha, inviting us over for dinner. 'You need a break from feeding the young ones on your own,' she said. 'Come on, it will take your mind off things.'

She had no idea how grateful I was to see her. I didn't let on just how grievous things had become with Kirsteen, but

I told her we would be setting off for London again at the crack of dawn.

It was a great weight off my mind not to have to worry about sorting out the boys' dinner, but I found it impossible to relax.

I've never known anyone's phone to ring more in one evening than my neighbour's did that night, and each time it did I froze, thinking it would be Jill. She knows this number, I thought. Something's gone wrong with Kirsteen.

By the end of the evening my nerves were shot to pieces. But the boys had had a good time, which was the main thing. The next few days would be hard for them, so I was glad to see them enjoy themselves.

The journey down to London was even more stressful. For six hours I was out of telephone contact, the words 'What if?' racing constantly through my mind. If I wasn't careful I'd drive myself mad.

MARTIN JR: I woke up that morning really excited because my whole class was due to go on a school trip. I was looking forward to it so much that I couldn't sleep. I remember getting up early and going downstairs. Dad was already dressed. He just said, 'I'm sorry, you won't be going on your trip. Kirsteen's taken a turn for the worse. We have to get back to London.'

Even though I was really disappointed, I was happy that I was going to see Mum again. That was the best thing about going down to London. I never really understood why we had to be there all the time – we weren't doctors, we couldn't help. But the thing that confused me most was not seeing Mum. At home we spent most of our time with her because Dad worked. So why was she always the one who had to stay in London? I hated leaving her there, although I knew that Kirsteen must want her as well. I didn't really appreciate how scared Mum must have been. I just knew I wanted her around a bit more.

I suppose it must have been the same when Kirsteen was at Yorkhill. I never really understood what the problem was back then. I knew that her bladder was on the outside of her stomach, but I didn't really know what a bladder was. I could see a red thing poking out where I didn't have anything, and I knew she was different, but I wasn't quite sure what was wrong with her. I also knew that Kenneth and I weren't allowed to play with her very much. But the worst thing for me was waking up some days and finding Mum or Dad missing. That happened quite a lot. Occasionally, they'd both be gone. I'd get out of bed and I wouldn't know where they were, and one of our neighbours would be sitting downstairs. 'It's all right, lad, your mum and dad have taken your wee sister to the hospital. I'll fix you some breakfast and they'll be back in no time.'

MARTIN: Eventually, we arrived at Euston and jumped into a cab. Half an hour later we were walking through the doors of Great Ormond Street. I was terrified of what I might find.

When I set my eyes on Kirsteen I had to do a double take. There was nothing of her. She was all skin and bones.

I think I was in shock. Jill had told me how bad things were but on the other end of the phone I'd always pictured my little girl as I remembered her when I left. The person lying in front of me was a stranger. She hadn't eaten for so long and weighed just one and a half stone.

I cursed myself for not having been there earlier.

The four of us sat there with Kirsteen. We had a lot of catching up to do. She barely had the strength to speak, but managed to say one thing to me: 'Dad, when I get out of here I need to eat – a lot!'

When Mr Ransley returned from his trip that same night he was mystified by the chain of events that had taken place in his absence. He wasted no time in clearing his diary for an emergency operation on Kirsteen.

'I've never seen anything like it,' he said. 'We're going to have to bite the bullet and go back in.'

He was fairly non-committal about what he was looking for, but it was obvious to everyone that something had to be done. Kirsteen's weight meant the operation would be a huge risk. We all knew it. But there was no choice. 'I've got to find out what's going wrong,' Mr Ransley said.

And I thought that if anyone had to do this operation I was glad it was him.

That trip down to theatre was the hardest ever. Kirsteen was so weak and so scared. She didn't want to go. As her bed was pushed out of the ward she began to scream.

'Save me! Save me! Don't let them kill me! I promise I won't do it again. Just take me home, I promise I'll be good.'

I was devastated. Absolutely desperate. The staff were marvellous and carried out their business very professionally. Kirsteen was attached to so much equipment that they struggled to get her bed into the lift. As the lift doors shut, I noticed a lovely nurse called Catriona, who would later become ward sister, and Fiona the Louise Ward play leader, leaning against each other. They were both distraught. I'd experienced this feeling before.

They weren't convinced Kirsteen would be coming out again.

JILL: Kirsteen cried and screamed all the way to theatre. The boys were still with us, but they waited outside the anaesthetic room with a nurse while Martin and I went in to see Kirsteen go under. It was the most heart-breaking sight. Watching Kirsteen's writhing body slump motionless made me feel sick. Her tiny little frame just twitched, and then it was still. I couldn't help but fear the worst.

Martin and I walked out of that room unable to speak to each other. We went to opposite ends of the corridor, tears streaming down our faces. I felt so useless. I couldn't even think of anything to say to my sons. There was nothing any of us could do. Then I noticed that the two nurses who had wheeled Kirsteen down were hugging each other, sobbing their hearts out. No one was saying it but we were all thinking the same thing.

Another nurse came over and handed me a pager. 'You can't do anything here,' she said. 'Get yourself a coffee. We'll bleep you if there is any news.'

I didn't want to go a yard out of sight of the theatre. The nurse was insistent, though. And she was right. I don't think we were helping anybody by being there. As she spoke I realised how drained I felt.

'Maybe we should,' I said to Martin.

The next three and a half hours were the longest of my life. We sat in the cafeteria not saying a word to one another or to the boys. Even they sensed the severity of the situation and just read quietly. Martin and I walked around, we sighed and we cried. But mainly we just stared at the pager.

You've never seen four people move so fast as when it bleeped.

Mr Ransley was waiting for us with a big smile on his face. As soon as I saw him I wanted to cry again, but he looked as calm as ever as he told us, 'The operation was a success. We can all relax now.'

Once we'd finished celebrating, he explained what he had done.

'It looks like I picked the perfect moment to go back in,' he beamed. 'And I'm pretty sure I've put it right now.' The problem wasn't the one he'd originally diagnosed. The fistula was never going to fix itself. As a result of all the operations Kirsteen had had earlier, there had been a partial breakdown of her bowel and intestine, as a result of which faeces was now being allowed to escape and find its way into her bladder through the holes made for the stent catheters. Mr Ransley had now removed what he himself described as 'that ropey tissue' from the equation and made good the repair.

When he finished his explanation by saying, 'I have now definitively fixed it and it will never be a problem again,' I could have kissed him.

CHAPTER 11

What if I Can't Do It?

KIRSTEEN: When you haven't eaten anything for a month you're bound to get hungry. More than that, you start to obsess about food. All the while I was being nourished by the Hickman line or another drip, I couldn't stop thinking about my favourite foods. Cake, lasagne, spaghetti, pizza.

The last thing I remember saying before Mr Ransley operated on me was, 'When I get out of here I need to eat.' Apparently I said lots of other things on the way to the theatre, but I don't remember those. Food was the main thing on my mind. I couldn't wait until I was well enough to eat properly.

I'm really lucky that Mr Ransley came back from his trip to Italy when he did. I honestly don't know if I would have lived for another week. It's a subject my parents and I never discuss. We're just grateful he returned that day.

When I came round after the operation I felt really sore in my stomach. Gradually, I realised my neck hurt as well.

I was told that Mr Ransley had fitted another Hickman line while I was under anaesthetic. 'This time,' he promised, 'there will be no problems.'

I was too sick to talk, but I believed him. I guess that means still no more food for a while, I thought.

Mr Ransley said it would take a while for my bladder to start growing and working. I would have to use catheters for the rest of my life, he said, and they would show me how to do it. I had to come to terms with the fact that I would never be perfectly normal. But there was one major improvement.

The nappies were gone.

That meant so much to me that I struggled to get my head around the idea. Mr Ransley said the new system he had installed would work perfectly with no more leaks. He promised me, in fact. I'd been in nappies all my life. I couldn't really imagine being without them.

'No one will be able to bully me any more,' I thought. That time, during the school play, when people had seen me getting changed was so horrible I'd wanted to curl up and die. But now I could get changed with everyone else.

There had been times when I'd thought I'd be in nappies for ever. Now, thanks to Mr Ransley, I felt free at last.

It was brilliant news, but I couldn't really take it in at the time because I still looked so ill. There were three tubes coming out of my stomach attached to large bags at my side. These were for drainage. It sounds horrible, but the tubes were permanently sewn into me. I couldn't pull them out if I'd tried.

'You'll have to keep these in for a few weeks, just until your wounds heal,' Mr Ransley explained. 'You won't recognise yourself afterwards.'

Mum and Dad were with me the moment I opened my eyes. I don't think I'd ever thought about it before but it was incredible how either one or both of them was always there for me. I was in that bed for five weeks. Every day Mum or Dad was sitting there next to me. Even when I was unconscious, they stayed. Even when I was sleeping there was usually one of them snoring in an armchair near by. The only time they left me alone was when they were asked to leave.

It didn't really make a difference which one of them was there, as long as someone was. It's when you're on your own that you get really scared. It's then you start to worry about worst-case scenarios – all the mistakes that could be made or the terrible things that might happen to you. I always thought that if something went wrong I wanted to be with my family.

Mostly, I wasn't well enough to talk to them, but I just liked the company.

My family understood this and were used to it; they would happily sit there reading or talking to other people, but some of my other visitors weren't so comfortable. I remember when one of my second cousins came in to see me. It was a lovely surprise when her family came by because they live so far away. She was about fifteen at the time and brought lots of magazines to show me. She was sitting there, turning the pages and chatting about the stuff in them, and I recall thinking, this is really nice but I cannot talk to her. I literally, physically, could not find the strength. After a while, I could see she began to feel awkward. But there was nothing I could do.

I felt so guilty because she'd travelled so far. I wished I could have told her that just by being there she had made my day. But I just felt so weak.

When I was younger it never occurred to me that my visitors might feel uncomfortable. I thought it was just me who was suffering. Before my last operation at Yorkhill, I remember being aware that people were next to my bed talking to me, but I was so tired, ill and even angry sometimes that I just couldn't always face answering them. You don't realise when you're lying there in pain that maybe they're not overjoyed to be in a hospital either. Also, some people feel really awkward and embarrassed on your behalf and don't know where to look when you have catheters and tubes sticking out of you.

I could tell after the operation that Mum was very nervous. I know I still appeared very sick, and although I didn't look any different from how I had before the operation, I had another Hickman line in my neck, external catheter bags tied to my legs again and I weighed the same as a one-year-old.

I didn't expect anything different. I never dreamed that I would wake up and be able to run around straight away. Even the thought of running made me feel nauseous, as I didn't have any energy. It wasn't as if there was a sudden realisation in my mind that I was better, or that I felt magically cured. But I wasn't in agony. It took me a while to register, but although my stomach felt sore, I didn't feel uncomfortable all over my body any more, like I had a poison running through me. And as the day wore on I thought: things are getting easier.

I didn't dare say it to anyone, even when the doctors told me I was getting better. I couldn't get too excited. After all, I'd heard it all before. At Yorkhill. I'd got used to them telling me I was better and sending me home, only to find out nothing had changed.

My main feeling after the operation was tiredness. Whenever I think of any of my stays in hospital, that's what I remember. I've got hundreds of memories of climbing into my hospital bed, knackered, and Great Ormond Street was no different. Your illness doesn't switch itself off at night and the nurses who worked through the night had to do the same checks on me as the daytime staff. I had to have blood tests twice a night, even on the first night after the operation, as they were anxious to make sure nothing went wrong with my new Hickman line. It was hard to sleep anyway because every time I moved I felt the catheter shift inside me. It was always like that. I always had things sticking out of me. There was always a tube or a catheter in the way. I'd try to get into a comfortable position to sleep but there'd be something digging into me, or I'd be worried I was going to damage something. Sometimes, I'd be crushing a tube without realising it and pressure would build up until I'd suddenly get uncomfortable and have to move again. I would usually lie awake most of the night then conk out for about two hours at dawn. And even then, if I did manage to drop off, I'd be woken up by nurses trying to take a sample from my foot without me noticing. It was a really exhausting time.

On the second day after my operation Mum and Dad said I looked so much better already. I don't know if they were just saying that to make me feel better. But I think I felt it.

It was then that I remembered my friend Alex. I hadn't seen him for days.

'Where is he?' I asked my mum. Although I was young, I think I feared the worst because I knew he had been very sick.

'He was discharged a few days ago,' she said. 'You were too ill to say goodbye.'

I was really sad when I heard that, but delighted that he was well enough to leave. The next day, though, Mum announced to me, 'You've got some visitors.'

I waited to see who it was. When I saw Alex and his dad walk into the ward I couldn't help smiling. We talked a lot about how horrible operations are and how we were looking forward to Christmas. Then Mum said that if we wanted, Alex was welcome to come and stay with us when I'd got my strength back. We always have a lot of guests at our house, so I knew she wasn't joking.

I had something else to look forward to as well. While I was recovering in Great Ormond Street I turned seven. I was still quite weak but Dad and my brothers had brought down lots of presents the last time they came so now I found the strength to open them.

And my good luck didn't stop there. The next day Mr Ransley came down and said that I was responding really well. 'If you carry on like this we'll have your Hickman line out tomorrow and start thinking about getting you out of here.'

I couldn't believe it. A few days ago I was at death's door. I didn't think I would ever be allowed home. And now they were talking about discharging me.

The only downside was the removal of the Hickman line. I knew it had probably saved my life because I was being fed by it. And I knew that once it came out I really was on the road to recovery. But I'd only just had a major operation – the idea of going back into theatre really upset me.

I got myself so worked up about it that I could hardly breathe. I think I stopped listening properly as well. On the day I was due to be seen again a nurse told Mum and me that there was an emergency and Mr Ransley had been called away. My operation would have to be postponed until the next day.

Mum said she needed to pop out for ten minutes. I think I must have fallen asleep because the next thing I remember is suddenly sitting bolt upright, confused, frightened – and convinced that my operation was happening in half an hour.

'Where's Mum?' I thought. 'She knows I'm having an operation, where is she?'

I began to panic. What if she doesn't come back in time? I'll have to go down for the operation on my own. I can't do it!

The thought of being alone when they wheeled me to theatre really brought home to me how wonderful my parents had always been. I started to pray: 'Please come back, and I promise I'll always be good.'

When you're young ten minutes can seem like hours. I started to get angry. I was just uncontrollable, sobbing, 'How could you leave me? How could you make me do this on my own?'

For a while I really thought I was going to have to say, 'I'm sorry, I don't want the Hickman line taken out. I want to keep it.'

I was in a terrible state when Mum came back into the room. She couldn't understand how I'd managed to get so worked up in the ten minutes she'd been gone. I explained what had upset me and she just hugged me as hard as she dared. 'I'd never leave you like that,' she said.

When I had the operation the next day, she was with me as usual, right up to when I was put under. When I woke up after the operation it was the same old story. I ached, I felt nauseous and my head was cloudy. If all these operations are supposed to make me feel better, I wondered, why do I always feel so much worse afterwards?

But this time I knew that I really was on the mend – and to prove it I was finally allowed to eat.

Having dreamed about food for so long, the first thing I said to Dad after my Hickman line was removed was, 'Take me to the café.' I hadn't eaten a thing for over four weeks. I was starving.

I was so frail that I had to be helped into a wheelchair, but I could hardly contain my excitement as Dad pushed me to the restaurant. I was already planning what I was going to have. As soon as we arrived, I ordered everything I could see and, before long, I had a mountain of food piled up on my tray.

'Are you sure about this?' Dad asked.

'I'm so hungry!' I said. 'This is just for starters.'

By the time Dad had wheeled me to a table I think I was actually salivating. I didn't know where to begin. I took a couple of bites out of a sandwich while I decided what to eat next.

But then something very odd happened to me.

I felt full. I hadn't realised that during the time I wasn't eating my stomach was getting used to it, and my appetite had effectively shrunk. Dad was shocked. He'd watched me waste away to almost nothing and here I was turning down food.

'Eat some more,' he urged me, but I couldn't. I just wasn't hungry.

'I'm too full.'

I'd been dreaming of eating for so long and now I had the chance I couldn't take it.

I began to wonder: would I ever be 'normal'?

JILL: After five weeks in hospital Kirsteen was allowed home. She was eating things like chicken noodle soup, ice cream – foods she could easily swallow – but she was still incredibly frail and all the tubes made her look more sick than she was. It was such a relief to be leaving Great Ormond Street. It wasn't quite the end, though.

'You'll need to come back in three weeks when the wounds have healed,' Mr Ransley said. 'We'll have those tubes and bags out and she'll be as good as new.'

It was wonderful news but it seemed a long way off.

Kirsteen was confined to a wheelchair so our trip home was very scary. We had decided to hire a car and drive the 400 miles to Milngavie. It seemed the best way to travel. I had been afraid Kirsteen's bags and the tubes could get torn during a train journey – and anyway, after so long in hospital we had accumulated too much luggage to carry.

The journey itself felt like it would never end, but as the signposted miles to Glasgow gradually got lower, I began to think of the light at the end of the tunnel. Lifting Kirsteen out of the car and into the house was an amazing landmark. It really felt like we were getting somewhere.

I didn't know it, but that was the start of three weeks of hell.

As far as Martin is concerned, that period down in Great Ormond Street was the worst of our lives. Kirsteen was more ill than she'd ever been. We could have lost her. It was horrendous. But we were surrounded by hundreds of amazing doctors and nurses and all the best medical technology in the world. It was scary, and I'd hardly got a moment's sleep for a month, but I had faith in the people around me.

When we came home, I was on my own.

I begged him not to but Martin had to go back to work the day after we got back. I know it wasn't his choice. He'd taken so much time off already as compassionate leave and holiday over the last five weeks that he couldn't afford to take another minute.

That is when it hit me just how much responsibility was resting on me. It would be just me and Kirsteen in our house and I was terrified I was going to do something wrong.

Kirsteen was healthier than she'd been two weeks earlier, but she still looked like something out of a concentration camp – so tiny and weak. Her arms and legs were like pencils. There was no flesh on her. You felt if you touched her she would have snapped. And the tubes coming out of her looked terrifying; they looked like part of her body because they were permanently sewn in, so it wasn't just something I could unclip when it was time for a bath or bed.

The more I looked at her, the more I wished Martin could have stayed home a bit longer, but it was impossible.

I knew that now, more than ever, Kirsteen needed me to be strong. But I really struggled. All the anxiety of the last month hit me at once. There was so much pressure.

The first few days were hell. I still had the boys to deal with, school runs, shopping and other errands. And wherever I went, Kirsteen had to go too. Most seven-year-olds run into the car and do up their own seatbelts. I had to carry Kirsteen, then struggle to strap her in. It's hard enough with a baby, but Kirsteen was so much bigger I barely had a spare inch to move or reach across her. She didn't weigh very much but her size really got in the way. And I was petrified of tangling up one of the delicate tubes or bags that were attached to her.

The first time I tried to get her into the car it took me half an hour. At the end of it I got into the driver's seat and burst into tears. I just sat there outside the house for a few minutes before I could move. I can't do it, I kept thinking. But I knew I had no choice.

Martin did as much as he could. He was always punctual coming home from work and, if he was passing during the day, he'd call in. He'd also come home for lunch if at all possible. I spent most of the first two days watching the clock, willing him to walk through the door. It was horrible.

I could see gradual improvements in Kirsteen's weight every day but the tubes never got easier to deal with. There was so much potential for injury or danger. Daytimes were hard enough, especially when the boys were around. They were banned from going near Kirsteen for three weeks. I felt terrible telling them that, but I had to protect her.

But bedtimes were the worst. There was no easy way to protect the tubes and keep the bags undisturbed. If you taped them down onto the bed then the tube might come out of the bag if Kirsteen moved about. If you didn't tape them onto the bed then the tubes were just loose. Who knew where they could go if she tossed and turned in the night?

On the second night my worst fears were realised.

After weeks of being by Kirsteen's bedside in hospital I didn't dare break the habit at home. We didn't have the luxury of nurses checking on her every few minutes so that was left to me. With so many other things to do, it was a struggle for me to keep this up. But I'm so glad I did.

Kirsteen had been in bed for an hour. I was just opening the door to check on her when I heard a noise I recognised. She can't breathe, I thought.

I burst into the room and flicked the lights on. Kirsteen was pulling anxiously at a tube that had become tangled around her neck. But the more she struggled, the more her weight pressed down on the tube. She was strangling herself.

'Oh my God! Kirsteen, what have you done?'

I lifted her head to unwrap the tube. She was gasping. Her face was white and her little fingers were digging sharply into the rubber hose. I hugged her to me. Then, after some coughs, she started to breathe properly.

'It's all right,' I said, 'Mummy's here.'

I'd got away with it this time. But what if I hadn't stopped by when I did? What if we weren't so lucky next time?

After the first week things began to get easier, but I could never truly relax. At least I knew, even in my darkest moments, there was light at the end of the tunnel. Mr Ransley was confident he'd done everything right. If I could just hold myself together enough to get through these few weeks then we'd soon be heading back down to London and then that would be it. The tubes would come out.

I had so much faith in Mr Ransley, and I think that is what dragged me through. As long as I believed in him, I told myself I could do it.

As I prepared to return to London with Kirsteen I dared to let myself think, 'The next time we come back to Milngavie she'll be better.'

It was odd going down to London without Martin but he needed to work and the boys had been disrupted enough. After the last three weeks I felt I could cope with anything. And the fact that Martin's mum and dad had generously paid for us to fly down this time meant the trip started on a really positive note. That upbeat mood continued throughout our journey, and there was a real sense of optimism when we arrived at Great Ormond Street. All our favourite nurses, Evelyn, Marika and so many others, came by to see us. I was given a bed in Kirsteen's room and was allowed to sleep next to her.

The second day after we arrived Mr Ransley took out the tubes. It was a momentous occasion for us. For once I had to remind myself that the general anaesthetic was still dangerous, but I was so excited about the future that I couldn't wait for her to go into theatre.

While I waited for Kirsteen to come round I was told that everything had gone to plan. The surgery on the bladder had taken hold, there were no leaks, no signs of the faecal trouble that she'd had before.

She would never be able to urinate normally, but that had never been the aim. The best Mr Ransley could do – the best anyone could do – was to construct her bladder to be big enough to hold as much urine as possible, before it was manually drained via a catheter inserted through a permanent hole in the tummy. Looking at Kirsteen, you would just think she had an extra belly button. I couldn't believe how perfect she seemed.

I remember the feeling I had had every time we walked out of Yorkhill. I would say to Martin, 'That's only until the next time. Our daughter is never going to get better.' Whenever we walked out of the hospital we were only at the end of a 'stage' and the doctors were always saying, 'Next time we see you we'll do this.' That's how it was.

Seeing her now though, knowing she would be ready to leave Great Ormond Street within a few days, I actually felt, for the first time in her life, that this was it. She looked normal and she would soon be able to act normal. I began to dream that she could live a regular life. I was as happy as I could be.

KIRSTEEN: I was as sore as usual after the operation to unplug the tubes and permanent drainage bags. It hurt to speak and if I coughed I thought I would burst. But I knew all that would pass. I'd had so much experience, I knew the pattern.

Mr Ransley said he was very pleased with how everything had gone, and said that there were two things he would like to see happen before I left. Number one was that he wanted to see me stronger and less reliant on my wheelchair. Yes, I thought. I want that as well.

But the second condition left me afraid.

'Now,' he said, 'you're going to have to learn to catheterise.'

The bag that he had disconnected had been collecting my urine without me needing to drain. But that was only ever going to be a temporary measure. Now I would have to learn to do it myself.

Ever since my Mitrofanoff procedure at Yorkhill, Mum and Dad had been able to plug a catheter into a tube that stuck out of my stomach in order to drain my urine. Every single one of those drains hurt – the first one more than anything. Even though I was only four at the time, I'll never forget my brother Martin wanting to call the police to rescue me.

All my bad memories of catheterising came flooding back at once. The thought of doing it again made me shake. I was scared. There wasn't even anything to plug into – I just had this weird hole in my stomach. I felt sick even thinking about doing it.

But the doctors were insistent that I had to learn to do it myself. They needed Mum to learn as well, but, I was told, 'You're staying here until you can do it yourself.'

I steeled myself, and in my head I kept saying, come on, you can do it, you can do it.

I held the catheter with one hand and used my other to locate the hole. It felt funny under my finger's touch. Taking a deep breath I lined up the tube from the catheter and pushed.

I got about two centimetres of the way in before the pain hit me.

'I can't do it!'

A nurse came over to help me. She tried to explain it as clearly as possible, and she didn't pull any punches.

'Right, we're going to go through a gate now,' she said as she pushed the tube in. 'Soon you'll be able to do this easily but this time it's going to really hurt you.'

And she was right. It did.

The pain was unbearable. Why was she doing this to me? I felt anger building up inside me. For every second the nurse was doing it I just wanted to kick her.

And less than two hours later I had to go through it again. For the next week or so I would have to catheterise every ninety minutes, but eventually I'd be able to last four hours between drains, and longer overnight.

My second attempt to do it myself was as much of an ordeal as the first. The third, fourth and fifth followed exactly the same pattern. But I had a plan. I'd worked out that if I kicked up a fuss someone else would do it for me. And I was right. Mum and the nurses would stand over me, I wouldn't put it in properly, then I'd stand up and it would fall out. 'Oh dear,' I'd say. Then they would do it for me. It sounds pretty childish – then again, I *was* only seven – but I couldn't think of any other way.

As the days passed I was put under more and more pressure. Sometimes it was just a nurse with me, but on one occasion I remember four doctors around the bed, all encouraging me to try it myself. I could feel how anxious they were for me to succeed, and for once I really tried. But I just couldn't bring myself to do it. Imagine sliding something into your own stomach? It seemed so unnatural to me. And what's more, I knew it was going to hurt.

In the end the doctors drifted away, one by one, and I was left with just Mum sitting there.

She was as disappointed with me as she was frustrated.

'Why didn't you at least try?' she asked. 'It's for your own good.'

'But it hurts too much,' I said. 'You don't understand.'

I could see she was upset and that made me feel guilty. But something strange happened while we were talking. I had the catheter tube in my hand and I was fiddling near the hole where it goes in. I wasn't really concentrating on what I was doing because I was too busy arguing with Mum. And then it happened.

'I've done it!' I realised. 'I've put it in.'

Poor Mum didn't know how to react. She was so relieved that I'd managed to do it on my own, but she was also angry. 'Why couldn't you have done this three days ago?' she demanded. 'Why do you put yourself, and me and all those poor doctors through all this?'

I didn't say anything. But I smiled as I realised how easy it had been to do. And how little it had hurt. Just a mild discomfort if anything.

All I could think of was what this meant. If I could do this, then I was on the way to being independent at last. I didn't need anyone else to do things for me. It was a huge achievement for me, but there were still other things I had to do before I could be discharged.

'We don't like patients leaving if they still need a wheelchair,' a nurse called Jo told me. 'But if we can get you walking a little bit you'll be able to go home.'

After so many days of staring at the same four walls, I was desperate for a change of scenery. And Jo used this boredom to inspire me.

'You can ask for a wheelchair all you like,' she said, 'but if you want to go down to the shop then you are walking there. No excuses.'

I think that was quite clever. Even though I knew every single thing they had for sale, looking around the hospital shop was one of the highlights of my day. Feeling so weak and sorry for myself it was always easier to let someone push me in a chair. But now Jo wanted me to walk.

'You'll thank me later,' she promised.

As I winced from the pain of putting my weight on one foot after the other, I seriously doubted that. But she was right. It took me nearly an hour the first time, but I got stronger and quicker. For the rest of the day she let me use the wheelchair but only after I'd managed to get downstairs under my own steam.

I can't help thinking that if it had been left to me, I might still be in bed now.

My doctor was so pleased with my recovery that he said I deserved a treat. Some of the patients were being taken to London Zoo for a day trip.

'If you feel up to it I think we can find a place for you,' he said.

I was so excited. But I still couldn't walk properly.

'Do you think I'll be able to go in my wheelchair?' I asked Mum.

'Of course you can,' she said.

I couldn't wait to have my first taste of fresh air after a week cooped up indoors. As the automatic doors at the main entrance slid open I noticed there were a lot more people than usual hanging around there. Then I saw that two men were carrying large cameras.

'What are they doing?' I asked the nurse who was pushing me.

'They're filming the hospital for a television advert,' she said. 'We're hoping to use it to raise money.'

It had never occurred to me that hospitals had to ask people for help. I had never given a minute's thought to where they got their money from. When you're young you don't think about things like that.

But I certainly didn't want to think about it then. I was just so happy to be outside, I couldn't help smiling. A second later I heard a voice call out.

It was one of the film crew. 'Excuse me,' he said. 'I hope you don't mind me asking, but I wondered if you would allow us to film you?'

I didn't know what to say. 'You'd be helping Great Ormond Street,' the man continued and, suddenly, my mind was made up. He had said the magic words: 'help Great Ormond Street'.

'What do I need to do?'

'All we want you to do is repeat what you just did,' he explained. 'When you came out of the hospital you looked so happy that you'll give hope to all the other children who need to come here. And when people watching television see you smile, perhaps they will feel like donating some money to the hospital.'

I was a bit nervous as I waited to be pushed out again but I just thought about helping the hospital. When the doors opened I smiled naturally, happy again to be outside.

By the time we were ready to go to the zoo I had lost interest in seeing the animals.

All I could think about was raising money for Great Ormond Street.

CHAPTER 12

God Wouldn't Have Done That

KIRSTEEN: After so many false starts, I don't know why I suddenly believed I was going to be OK from now on. But I did. By the time we were ready to leave Great Ormond Street I was beginning to feel better. I had put a bit more weight on and I could walk further without the wheelchair. Mum said, 'I can't even recognise you as the same little girl who came here a week ago.'

I was sad to say goodbye to all my friends on the nursing staff, the doctors, and especially Mr Ransley. I couldn't thank them enough. I was too shy to really express myself, but I think my tears told them how grateful I was! I'm convinced they saved my life. I owe everything to the people at that hospital.

As well as being so talented and lovely, the nurses and

doctors at Great Ormond Street seemed to care more about their work than I was used to. My dad remembers both hospitals that treated me and he says there is no comparison. He told me, 'The nursing staff at Yorkhill would spend time standing about chatting, coats on ready to leave on the dot when their shifts finished. But at Great Ormond Street they never seemed to finish on time. They were always working, getting on with things.' That's exactly how I remember it. If a nurse started looking after me and I was due to go into surgery, she wouldn't leave me until I was out again. Some of them missed their lunch and sat with me during their breaks.

They didn't have to, but they did.

Dad had planned for me and Mum to travel home by train as usual, but my granddad very kindly stepped in and offered to pay for the return flight. And as it turned out, it was lucky he did. The train we would have caught otherwise was derailed just outside Glasgow. Several passengers suffered minor injuries. I got goosebumps when I thought I could have been among them.

Even though we were planning to fly, Mr Ransley was worried about how I would get home safely. He didn't want my bladder to get full and he didn't want me to have to attempt to drain during the journey.

'You'll need to catheterise every couple of hours, just for a week or so,' he said. 'But we don't want you worrying about that before you're even home.'

So just before I left a nurse plugged a large catheter inside my bladder and then taped it down the side of my tummy so it didn't become dislodged during the flight. Then it could fill gradually throughout the day, without me having to do anything. All I needed to be aware of was not damaging the bag.

'As soon as you get home you need to take the tube out, throw the bag away, and then begin draining every two hours,' she told me.

The journey was quite exciting. Mum just kept saying, 'It's brilliant,' every time she looked at me. Even though I wasn't a hundred per cent I was buzzing with the possibility of really being on the mend. By the time I was back in my own home I dared to believe that it had actually worked. After seven years of pain my problems might really be over.

It took me only a few days to realise that I'd already forgotten what it was like to be wrapped in a nappy, although the mental scars remained, and all those taunts at school will never leave me. I still needed to catheterise though. At first I was upset that this was something that would always be with me. But my friend Inya (Jane Wallace's daughter) cheered me up when she said, 'Catheterising is just like getting your ears pierced. At first it hurts like hell. But after that it's no bother. You don't even notice it's there.'

I remember thinking she was right, and I still remember those words even today, whenever I have to do it.

Getting back into some sort of normal routine was really important to me. My brothers were a bit wary of coming near me at first, but they soon saw that I was getting back to my old self. As soon as Martin and I had our first argument, he knew that I was better.

'Welcome back,' he said.

MARTIN JR: When you're young and of a similar age to your siblings, you're always squabbling about something. I don't think Kenneth did so much, but I had the normal brother/sister arguments with Kirsteen and she'd hit me just like any other sibling. But I couldn't really get back at her. I can remember Mum and Dad telling me to be gentle with her, and I'd always get into a lot more trouble than my sister did; I think she liked that!

We'd argue about everything. We still do. There's one thing that always winds us both up. The way our house is set up, there's a door to the shower room that leads from Kirsteen's room. So she basically has a shower in her room. If I want to use the shower I have to ask her. Normally it's all right, but if we've been arguing the night before, she'll just say, 'No.' If I'm quick I can get in and lock the door before she stops me. If I'm too slow she'll attack me on the way in and then I just have to bolt out again. And when she gets her hands on you she leaves scars!

Whenever we are messing around or she's trying to attack me, I am always subconsciously aware that her stomach is off limits. I've never thought about trying to hit her there, not even jokingly. If she's really in a rage I just have to hold her arms until my brother or my dad comes along and calms her down. But she'll never let it go unless she's hit me. She'll never stop unless she's got the last punch.

KIRSTEEN: It wasn't long before I had to think about going back to school. I had missed a lot of lessons, so I was anxious to catch up. I couldn't help feeling nervous though.

'Where do I say I've been?' I asked Mum.

'Just tell the truth. You were sick, but now you're better.'

I had plenty of friends, like everyone else, but I had never really confided in anyone as to the extent of my problems. In the back of my mind I knew that I would have to, and I began to practise what I would say as soon as I started back at school. I worked it out carefully: 'I was born with a condition which left my bladder on the outside of my body. It's all resolved now and my bladder's back inside my body so there's nothing really that you'd notice. I'm normal now, just like you.'

I even came up with a way to explain having to catheterise. I'd tell people that I just have to take some medicine every two hours. I didn't really want to go into detail in case it freaked my friends out. I was aware that even though I considered it normal and was dealing with it, other people might not be so open-minded. To this day, a lot of my friends still don't know the truth.

I can't begin to express just how confident I felt walking into school not wearing a nappy. I usually managed to drain on my own throughout the day without a problem. I would just ask my teachers – who were all female – for permission to go to the medical room, and they would always know what I meant.

On one occasion, however, we had a male supply teacher for the day. When it was time for me to drain, I put up my hand, as usual, and said, 'Excuse me, sir, I've got to go the medical room.'

'Why?' he asked. He clearly hadn't been briefed.

I wasn't expecting that, so I went really quiet. All of my nightmares suddenly came flooding back. The last thing I wanted to do in front of the whole class was to say that I had to drain, so I said, 'I just have to go.'

He didn't like that one bit. 'You're not going unless you tell me why,' he said.

As soon as I heard that I burst into tears. If I sat there for too long I would make myself really ill. My bladder would start to burn and I'd get stomach cramps. But I didn't want to embarrass myself in front of all my friends by admitting the truth.

As soon as he saw me crying, I think the teacher started to feel awkward. He didn't even try to stop me when I got up and ran towards the door.

I don't think it was his fault; the headmistress should have told him. But I did really feel betrayed at that moment. I was trying to fit in and everyone seemed to want to make me feel different. Still, I was determined not to let them, not then, nor when I started secondary school a few years later, although then I would be up against different problems.

Six months after my final operation at Great Ormond Street I had to go back for a check-up. Since I hadn't suffered any side effects or bad reactions, to my knowledge, Mum and Dad thought it would just be a formality. This time it was Dad who took me. We went on the overnight sleeper so that we wouldn't have to use one of the hospital's Trust houses. Dad didn't want to take anything away from someone whose need was greater than ours.

I was really happy to see everyone at the hospital. Lots of my favourite nurses were working when we arrived and it was great to catch up. Mr Ransley was really delighted with me. When you're the patient you don't think of yourself like others do. I'd just been trying to do as much as I could because I always wanted tomorrow to be better than today. But unbeknown to me my doctors obviously had a number of expectations – and I'd met every one of them.

'I really must be getting better,' I thought – and, for once, believed it.

We were due to leave for Milngavie that evening, but before we went Mr Ransley asked us for a favour. He explained that there was a little girl in the hospital – 'another one of these cases where I have to take it back to the beginning before I can repair the child' – whose family he'd like me to meet. So we went upstairs and were introduced to a nice young couple. Their daughter was about eighteen months old and had bladder exstrophy. The mum was in tears. Apparently, Mr Ransley thought their daughter's condition was a lot worse than they'd been told by their local hospital. This had come as a huge blow to them. They'd thought that coming down to Great Ormond Street was normal procedure and were flabbergasted when Mr Ransley put so bluntly what he felt.

I remember the father talking to Dad. He told him, 'Mr Ransley just came down to see us and he's left us shocked. He looked at our daughter's notes from our old hospital, then he looked at our little girl and he said, "I'm really sorry, I don't know how to break this news to you, but I wouldn't recognise your child as being the subject of these notes. And, I'm afraid to say, I'm going to have to take her back to nothing and start again."'

I can't imagine how they must have felt. They'd watched their daughter going through operations for a year, all the while thinking progress was being made.

I believe that Mr Ransley and his team have since campaigned for other hospitals to leave bladder exstrophy cases either to Great Ormond Street or one or two other specialist hospitals.

While I tried to cheer the little girl up, Dad tried to reassure her parents that they were in the very best hands. He told them something a lady called Brid Carr (one of the clinical nurse specialists in the urodynamics department at Great Ormond Street) had said to highlight the difference between Great Ormond Street and any other hospital: 'If you had a Rolls-Royce you'd want it serviced by the best mechanics, wouldn't you?'

MARTIN: We met a lot of people during our time in London. Kenneth says he loves the atmosphere in hospitals because he remembers how wonderful it was at Great Ormond Street. As a direct result of the experience he plans to become a doctor and specialise in Kirsteen's condition.

It doesn't matter who you are at Great Ormond Street, you're all in it together, so everybody helps each other, even if you've only just met.

One particular mother down there, whose son had spina bifida, really made Jill laugh. Seeing how worried Jill was, she said, 'You know what you need? Cannabis! I have to do it,' she went on. 'It's the only way you'll ever get through things. I couldn't cope without it.'

Everyone was different but we all just pulled together, each of us a shoulder for the other to lean on.

I remember one wee girl from Ireland who would bite and kick and lash out at the nurses when they tried to take away her catheter tubes. She was so distressed it broke your heart to watch. Her mother was at the end of her tether. In the end she grabbed her coat and said to me, 'I've got to get out. I can't take any more. You'll have to look after my daughter for a while.'

But we all had times like that. Times when the stress and the heartache just got too much to bear.

Part of the 'deal' if your child is admitted to Great Ormond Street is that the hospital will subsidise or pay for your travel to and from the building if you're not local. Plus, for those who were not local, there was the Trust house accommodation. We were always very grateful for a roof over our heads, but as far as travelling to and from London was concerned, we always paid our own way, even if it meant the occasional helping hand from my parents. It just seemed to be the right thing to do. The hospital needs to save all the money it can, and the way we looked at it, rather than paying for flights for us, they could be putting the money towards treating a poorly child.

We didn't want to take a single penny off Great Ormond Street unless we really had to.

Most other people also seemed to be very good about this, but we did meet the odd family whose approach was to take a cab instead of a bus, or a plane instead of a train. 'You're entitled to it,' they would say. 'You're entitled to get it free.'

'How are we entitled?' I wondered. 'What have we – or they – done to be entitled?' It seemed wrong for anyone to be so grabbing after all the hospital has done for them and their child.

There were times when we could have made it a lot easier for ourselves, but I just didn't want to take advantage. When the boys and I were travelling down for Kirsteen's seventh birthday we had her presents with us, our luggage and a great big presentation cheque from the Scots Women's Guild. I'd done some photography for them at the local church and I'd refused to take a fee. 'Just give a donation to Great Ormond Street,' I'd said. So they handed me £400 and the giant cheque so they could get a picture of Kirsteen with it for their newsletter. I was very happy to do it, even though Kirsteen was so ill at the time, but it didn't make our journey any easier.

I was lucky with a few charity photography jobs like that. And every penny I made went to the hospital in Kirsteen's name. What would be the point in raising money for them on one hand and then taking it back with the other, I always thought.

JILL: It's funny the people you meet and the different ways they have. After Kirsteen was born, I remember wondering why it was that I'd done everything right in my pregnancy, yet there people who take drugs and have perfectly healthy children. I mentioned this to a friend who is a regular churchgoer. She looked me in the eye and said: 'Imagine if Kirsteen had been born into a family in Easterhouse [a run-down part of Glasgow with a bad reputation]. What would have happened to her if she'd had drug addicts for parents?'

Thinking like that can help to put everything into perspective.

The problems with Kirsteen's friend from hospital, little Alex, really helped in that respect as well. He was such a brave boy and I had loved watching him recover in Great Ormond Street while we were there.

When we were first home with Kirsteen, I stayed in touch with his parents and, as I'd promised, we arranged for him to come up to stay with us during the Easter holidays.

But the week before Alex was due to come we got a phone call from his father. I'll never forget it for the rest of my life.

'Alex won't be able to come up next week,' he said. 'The doctors have found eight tumours in his lungs. He only has forty-eight hours to live.'

I couldn't believe it had all happened so quickly. That's the evil thing about cancer. It goes away and hides and then comes back when you think you're all clear.

Alex's parents had turned down further treatment because they said it was only delaying the inevitable and they didn't want him to suffer any more. He died soon after.

It seemed like half the hospital staff turned out for his funeral, among them our nurse friends Evelyn and Marika, who read out a letter from us. It's so typical of the hospital. To them he wasn't just a patient. He was a friend. They had got to know wee Alex. They had got to care.

A short while later I remember being on the phone to Alex's poor mum. I was crying my eyes out when I suddenly heard a noise behind me. It was Kirsteen. There were tears in her eyes as she marched right past me, into the kitchen, and threw her children's Bible into the bin.

Like a lot of adults raised in Christianity, we don't actively not believe, but religion doesn't play a role in our everyday lives. However, all schoolchildren in Scotland are given a Bible to help with their basic religious education. When I'd hung up the phone I asked Kirsteen what she was doing.

'I don't believe in God any more,' she said.

'Why not?' I asked. I couldn't help thinking that she was a little young to be making such decisions.

'Well, if there's a God he wouldn't have done that to Alex,' she said.

I didn't know what to tell her. Things like that do cross your mind when you see your own baby suffering, even if you're not a regular churchgoer. But surely a seven-year-old shouldn't be thinking that way?

'If there's a God,' she went on, 'why did he make Alex go through all those operations if he knew he was going to die in the end anyway?'

And to that I had no answer.

CHAPTER 13

You've Just Embarassed Me

KIRSTEEN: Apart from the fact that I have to return to Great Ormond Street once a year, I would call myself normal now. Yet a few years ago I couldn't have dreamed of the day when I would say that.

When I was younger I would sometimes think strangers could tell there was something different about me just looking at me, but I realise now that was silly. Dad tells everyone, 'To look at Kirsteen you'd never know what she's been through,' and I think he's right.

We had some nice holidays in the years after my final operation – we even went abroad a couple of times. I think some people expect me to be self-conscious about my scars and cover myself up, but I'm not ashamed. I wear what I like, even if I'm on the beach. And lots of people have scars.

People don't need to know what mine are for. They are a part of me now. They're part of who I am.

Looking back, my recuperation was quite a slow process. I was so small when I had that last operation, and my weight had dropped so much, but in the months and years that followed, I felt myself grow physically and mentally stronger.

By the time I was eleven I was like a different person. I was no longer afraid of other people, or what they thought. I was so much more confident than I'd been a few years before – and it was all down to how I felt about my body. I'm OK, I thought. I'm normal. And so what if I needed to drain? No one would suspect it just looking at me.

I had all the confidence in the world. As far as the rest of the world was concerned, there was no reason for me to stand out.

But then I had to start secondary school – and all that changed.

There have been occasions when I've felt that people were trying to alienate me on purpose. But sometimes, it was the ones who were trying to help me that caused the most pain.

When I joined the Douglas Academy I was eleven years old and I'd been catheterising on my own for four years. I know the education authorities were only trying to do the right thing, but somewhere along the line my feelings were put aside – and I suffered.

I'd had a brilliant special needs teacher at primary school who changed my nappies and sometimes helped me drain if I didn't go home for lunch. Most people at the school knew me because we were all from the same area. Whenever I'd been in hospital, my friends took just my absences for granted and made a big fuss of me when I got back. Mum would keep their parents up to date about my progress, but didn't really want anyone worrying too much.

But at secondary school I had a hard time. The school made quite a big deal about my welfare, and insisted on getting me a special needs teacher. They thought it was for the best, but I was really unhappy with the arrangement. I didn't want anyone to think I was different. I hate the idea of special treatment. I try to get by as best I can and all I want is for others to let me do that.

By trying to single me out for preferential treatment they actually made me feel lonely.

My special needs teacher at secondary school wasn't with me full time. She was just there to make sure I didn't get hurt between lessons. Even though my bladder was as 'fixed' as it was going to be, it's still a fragile area for me. An accidental elbow in my stomach could cause damage and affect how I catheterise. It's a slim risk, but one the school wasn't prepared to take, with hundreds of kids jostling one another in narrow corridors as they went to and from lessons. That meant I couldn't go into the canteen unaccompanied in case I got pushed, and so was usually taken in before anyone else. And I had to leave classes ten minutes before the end so I could walk to my next lesson down an empty corridor. At play times my teacher would go out and make sure I didn't play anything that involved running around.

And all of this just made me stick out.

I could appreciate what everyone was trying to do, but it was really embarrassing. Sometimes my special needs teacher would march into my lesson and say, 'Kirsteen, it's time to drain,' which was completely unnecessary as I would know it was time to leave as soon as I saw her at the door.

The funny thing was, the special needs teacher was a bit squeamish about the whole thing. I think it freaked her out. In the end, I realised she was allowing more and more time for me to get out of lessons and drain, so as to make doubly sure nothing went wrong.

All the kids who didn't know me had no idea what the teacher was talking about. I heard from my friends about all the questions that were going around:

'What's this about needing to drain?'

'Where does Kirsteen go?'

'Why does she need a special needs teacher?'

'What's wrong with her?'

'Who does she think she is?'

After a few weeks, I began to find it difficult to pay attention in class. I would sit there staring at the door, dreading the moment when my bodyguard would burst in.

Another problem was that by leaving each lesson early, I would miss the point at which the teachers dished out the homework assignments. My friends tried to keep me up to date but sometimes they got the facts wrong and that dropped me into trouble.

I was also missing out on all of those moments when kids gossip and chat in between lessons. I was kept away from all that by being made to walk on my own.

I had been so excited about going to high school, just like my friends, but now I felt like an outsider.

Every night I went home and complained to Mum and Dad. They kept saying, 'It's for your own good. We only want you to be safe.' But after a while, it got so distressing that I didn't want to go to school any more. At that point my parents decided to act.

Dad went to see the headteacher and said he wanted the

special treatment to stop. But the school refused. In the end he had to write a disclaimer to the school, to the effect that if anything happened to me at school it would be my parents' – not the school's – responsibility.

At first, I regretted the decision and found myself jumping at my own shadow as I made my way between lessons with the rest of the crowd. But then I started to calm down and eventually I stopped thinking about it at all.

I was a 'normal' schoolkid at last.

One of the ways I try to live a normal life is by having as many hobbies as I can. I don't mind anyone seeing my scars, and as long as the hole where my catheter tube goes in is safe, that's the main thing.

I've also always liked music. Kenneth plays the bagpipes but I didn't fancy learning those. Apart from anything else, they're so heavy. So when the school gave me the opportunity to learn an instrument, I picked the flute. When I was ten I was taken to see the world-famous flautist James Galway in concert. One of his assistants knew of my illness and so I was invited backstage to meet him. I couldn't believe it when he asked if I wanted to play a duet with him. If Dad hadn't taken a picture I might have thought I was dreaming.

The Douglas Academy is quite renowned for its music school, apparently the best in Scotland, and as I'm not allowed to do PE at school (I think it has something to do with health and safety concerns) I go there during the PE period and practise my flute.

As much as I hate to be singled out for special treatment, when I sat there with James Galway that day it dawned on me that perhaps my story makes people take a bit more notice of me than they otherwise might. On this occasion I personally benefited because I got to play my flute with him.

But, I realised, perhaps I could use my experiences to help other people?

Looking back, that was a turning point in my life.

One moment that will always stick in my memory is when the television cameraman outside Great Ormond Street told me that the hospital needed help to raise funds. The advert I appeared in had been broadcast every Christmas since I left. Every time anyone saw it they would call me and say, 'I saw you on telly last night.' And every one of those people would know how important Great Ormond Street was. 'But,' I thought, 'there must be something more I can do.'

Like a lot of young girls – and their dads! – I was (and still am) a big fan of the television presenter Cat Deeley. At the time, *Stars in Their Eyes* was my favourite programme. I knew that Cat was a patron of Great Ormond Street so I thought I'd write to her for ideas. I sat down in my bedroom and composed a letter explaining that I would really like to help Great Ormond Street somehow because they'd saved my life, and asking whether she had any ideas as to how I could do it. Then I put it in an envelope and posted it to the hospital.

A few weeks later I got a phone call from the fundraising department at the hospital.

'We're so happy you would like to help us,' said one of the lovely ladies who works there. 'Would you be interested in coming down to an event we're holding in London at the Hard Rock Café?'

Of course I agreed instantly. The only downside was the fact that they wanted me to speak there.

I felt my stomach turn at the prospect.

The event was an awards ceremony for winners of Write4GOSH – a competition in which the *Sunday Times'*

Funday Times section had invited children to write stories for patients at Great Ormond Street Hospital (GOSH).

I spent ages worrying about what I was going to say.

'Just tell everyone what happened to you and how grateful you are to Great Ormond Street,' Mum said. 'As long as you speak from the heart people will like you and they'll listen.'

I put a few words onto paper and showed them to Dad, who made a couple of suggestions. Then I rewrote it and sent it to the hospital for approval.

'It's perfect!' came the response.

Now all I had to do was read it out in public.

As the event grew closer I discovered just how high profile it was going to be. Dad travelled down with me, which was good because he's great in these situations. I was taken over to meet the person who would be introducing me that day. It was Michael Aspel! It was incredible meeting someone so famous, and he was really friendly.

Then I felt my head spin as I saw who else was there. There was an actress called Sheila Hancock and the children's writers Michael Morpurgo and Jacqueline Wilson (author of the brilliant *Tracy Beaker* stories). I was really excited to meet all of them, but nothing compared to seeing my idol Cat Deeley standing just behind them. The lady from GOSH introduced me and I was speechless when I realised Cat knew who I was.

'I got your letter,' she said. 'I wanted to tell you you're a really brave girl, and I think it's great that you want to help the hospital to help other people.'

After I'd posed for some photographs with the celebrities and listened to some speeches, it was my turn to take to the stage. My stomach felt like it was doing somersaults, but I knew there was no turning back now. 'You can do this,' I thought.

All my powers of concentration were called upon to block out my fear. Before this, the biggest audience I'd ever spoken in front of was for Burns Day at my primary school when I'd had to read a poem out. Now I gritted my teeth and went for it. I was helped by Cat standing there encouraging me, sticking her thumbs up and mouthing things like, 'You're doing great' whenever I looked over.

Five minutes later it was over and I was being applauded by a hundred people. I can't really remember much about it because I was so anxious, but Dad filmed the whole thing on our video camera, and he told me I'd done brilliantly.

'You really did yourself proud up there,' he said. 'No one in this room can doubt how much Great Ormond Street means to you.'

Dad wasn't the only one who was impressed. One of the GOSH organisers, a lady called Sarah Hope, came running over as soon as the awards had been distributed.

'Kirsteen, that was wonderful,' she said. 'If you're interested, we have another event coming up soon and I'd love it if you could come and speak at that. I have to warn you though, it's a slightly bigger affair.'

That, I soon learned, was an understatement.

Every year, just before the summer Silverstone Grand Prix, a black tie ball is held to raise money for charity. In July 2004, the chosen charity was Great Ormond Street, and it has been ever since.

I didn't really know anything about Formula One, but Dad was really excited as we drove down to Banbury in Oxfordshire. To keep my mind off the prospect of making a speech I thought about how I'd be seeing Kerry Katona. She'd just won *I'm a Celebrity Get Me Out of Here* and all my school friends were talking about the fact that I was going to meet her.

We were greeted by Sarah Hope, Clare Cook (the organiser) and Harriet Powner, who has become one of my main contacts and a great friend. They took us through to a champagne reception inside the giant marquee that had been erected in the grounds of Stowe School. I could tell as soon as I walked in that there were a lot of important people there – important rich people, in particular.

The lawn of the school was covered with F1 cars. They looked really colourful and I was totally impressed even though I had never seen a race before!

Inside, the marquee was even more stunning. Everywhere I looked there were faces I recognised – Kerry Katona and her then-husband, Westlife singer Brian McFadden, and actors from *Holby City* and other TV programmes. Dad was really happy to meet Eddie Jordan and a few other racing legends. It was a spectacular event. From the sparkling chandeliers to the beautifully decorated tables, the event shouted 'luxury'.

We were treated just like all of the millionaire guests who had paid a fortune for their tickets, and were served an amazing-looking meal. Dad seemed to tuck in without a problem but I couldn't eat a thing. I was too nervous.

'What if I make a mistake in front of all these people?' I thought. I'd never seen such a big crowd. Before I left home Mum had said, 'Well, you did fine at the first one,' and I just had to remember that. But this was a huge step up from Write4GOSH – from a hundred people there to two thousand here.

I'd made a really big effort to perfect this speech. Dad had helped out with the structure but the words were mine. They have to be otherwise I don't think I could sound convincing saying them. I need to look natural when I'm on stage, and

I don't think I could do that if I was trying to read somebody else's words.

As I was being introduced after dinner, I felt all those nights of practising disappear in a puff of smoke. I looked out at all the celebrities in front of me, and panic set in. But then I looked back at my speech; I remembered saying the words over and over again at home, and I smiled.

The next few minutes flew by. I was surprised to find I was really comfortable up there, and when I had finished I got a standing ovation from everyone in the room. It was incredible.

When I got back to the table I saw that Dad had been videoing the proceedings. 'You did brilliantly,' he said. 'I'm so proud.'

Clare Cook from Great Ormond Street came over and said, 'Well done. There is a tear in everyone's eye.'

I was really happy that it had all gone so well from my own point of view, but hearing that the fundraising team thought so too meant the world to me.

After the speeches there was a charity auction. Most of the prizes were donated by insiders from Formula One, so they were the kind of things that money can't usually buy. One was a tour of the Silverstone Pit Lane – with Michael Schumacher as your guide! Even I had heard of him, and was so impressed that someone as important as him was putting himself out to help Great Ormond Street. It just showed me how prestigious the hospital is worldwide. Another prize was the chance to ride in a two-seater Minardi car. I remember thinking that was a really cool prize; sadly, I didn't have the thousands of pounds it took to outbid everyone else!

I couldn't get over the enormous sums that were being offered by the audience. Dad said it was 'silly money', but all I knew was that Great Ormond Street deserved every penny.

As the auction went on, I saw that Dad was getting agitated. I was worried that he wanted to go home. On the contrary, not only did he want to stay, he wanted *me* to get involved again.

'How would you feel about auctioning your autograph?' he asked me. 'The audience really seemed to like you. You might get a few hundred pounds.'

I thought he was mad, but said, 'Why not? If you think it will work, let's do it.'

I watched him go over to Sarah Hope and cringed when she gave him the same bemused look that I had. At that moment I wished the ground would swallow me up. I couldn't bear the thought of her laughing at me, or saying, 'What were you thinking of? Who would pay money for your autograph?'

But then her expression changed, as though something had just occurred to her. She grabbed Dad's elbow excitedly and said something to him. Then off she went.

Dad walked back to the table giving me the thumbs-up sign. I don't know what I really thought would happen but the process was in motion. Now it was just a question of how embarrassing it was going to be!

It wasn't long before the auctioneer announced that they had a special prize. Suddenly, it hit me just what I had agreed to, and even Dad was beginning to look anxious. He admitted to me afterwards to thinking that if this idea bombed now he'd have traumatised his own child.

I was asked to join the auctioneer. I hadn't expected that! My heart was in my mouth. It seemed to take for ever to climb the five or six steps up to the stage; I was so nervous I didn't think my legs would carry me that far.

But what happened next was like a fairytale. If Dad hadn't recorded it, I think I still wouldn't believe it today.

The auctioneer was excellent at his job and the audience had been very generous so far, but still I thought that if we raised £500 then that would have been good.

Within minutes, though, the bidding was up to £3000.

It was incredible. Three, five, seven, nine, £10,000 – still it went up. But it didn't stop there – £11,000, £12,000. Now it was up to £15,000. I thought it couldn't go further than that. But it did.

I'd never even imagined that kind of money before. It lost a lot of meaning for me at this point, but some people obviously knew what it meant.

My signature finally sold for £20,000.

I was astonished. Dad was astonished. The GOSH fundraisers were astonished. Even people like Kerry and Brian came up to me afterwards and said they were astonished too!

The successful bidder asked to remain anonymous but I met him afterwards to sign my name for him and he was a lovely man. He just said, 'It was worth it to help such a good cause and a wonderful young lady.'

I've never felt so proud in my life.

I got quite a bit of publicity for that event. Lots of newspapers and magazines wanted to write about the girl who had sold her signature for £20,000. I felt really odd talking to people about myself, though; it was Great Ormond Street I wanted to talk about.

Then, one day, I was asked if I would appear on a television programme, and thought this was my chance to really get some publicity for the hospital. Whenever I had seen the Trisha programme it was normally very noisy with lots of people arguing with one another. But on the day I was invited to appear Trisha was concentrating on people who had really uplifting stories to tell.

I was worried beforehand that the audience might be unkind to me, but everyone was lovely. And I was so happy that I got the chance to tell millions of people about the good work of Great Ormond Street. Afterwards, we were driven all the way home from the studios in Norwich in a taxi. I was asleep before we'd gone ten miles.

But there were drawbacks to my experiences with the media. I'd had to get permission to miss school for a day when I went to the Hard Rock Café and the Trisha show. My teachers were happy for me to go because it was for a good cause. But it never occurred to me that I would get a few strange looks the next day.

I remember being in a wheelchair years ago, and my mother pushing me to pick my brothers up from school in Craigdhu. I couldn't help noticing how many children were staring at me as if I had two heads. My mum told me to ignore them, but it made me feel really uncomfortable.

For some reason, it felt just like that the day after I'd met some celebrities. I was aware that quite a few people were starting to avoid me. I was made to feel alienated just because I'd met famous people and they hadn't. I tried really hard not to boast about what I'd done and who I'd met, because it was the cause that was most important to me. But when my friends asked me what Cat Deeley or Kerry Katona or someone else was like, I would tell them, and then other people would get annoyed.

I even fell out with one of my closest friends over it. It sounds so silly. She accused me of some horrible things. 'You think you're better than us because you've met Cat Deeley.' But I really didn't.

Mum told me they were just jealous, but it still hurt. I talked to a friend of my big brother Kenneth about it and he agreed. 'It's definitely just jealousy,' he said. 'I know some of those girls and it's not personal. They just can't stand the fact you've done something that they want to do.'

I began to panic that when I appeared on television a few days later they would hate me even more. Maybe they thought I was becoming famous and they didn't want that to happen to one of their friends? But I was only meeting celebrities. I wasn't one myself. I was still the same person they had always known, and all I wanted to do was say 'thank you' to the hospital that had done so much for me.

It's a lot better now. If anyone is still jealous they hide it well. It took a bit of getting used to but now my friends just like hearing about the people I've met and getting all the gossip. Apart from that, I'm not treated any differently.

It was only a couple of months before I was invited to attend another event – this time even further away from home in St Helier, Jersey. It was a special fundraising party called the Peter Pan Ball. The whole thing was organised by a lady called Caroline Strachen, whose daughter Catherine became a good friend that weekend.

Before the event, I had lunch with Carole Smillie and Cherie Lunghi at Jersey Zoo. They were both really interesting to talk to and they happily had their pictures taken with me. Then we went back to the Hotel de France for the ball where I would have to give another speech.

Mrs Strachen did an incredible job. The stage was in the shape of a ship and the waiters and waitresses were all dressed as pirates. The guest of honour that night was the Duchess of Gloucester and I got to meet her in the official line-up. I just had to phone home to tell Mum that because I knew she would be impressed.

A few weeks later, I met another member of royalty, Sophie Wessex, at the Great Ormond Street Carol Service in Kensington, London. Peter Pan was meant to have lived in Kensington Park, so I think that is why they chose that area. I was introduced to the congregation inside St Paul's Church by Sir Trevor MacDonald, and I also met Betty Boothroyd, Bill Bryson and Julian Fellowes there.

But one of my favourite events was in June 2005. I don't think it raised any money, and I didn't see many celebrities there, but it was easily the most important function I'd been invited to.

After many years of wonderful work helping people like me, Mr Ransley was retiring. The party was held at a hotel in London so Jane Wallace said Dad and I could stay with her and Inya. It was really great to see my friend again and we were both determined to see Mr Ransley off in style. The party was incredibly moving. About a hundred of Mr Ransley's patients were there, past and present, some with their families.

I was surprised to see a few fairly old people – and really comforted that they'd enjoyed normal lives despite being born with bladder exstrophy. I spoke to dozens of people I'd never met before. It was a unique experience for us all, and it was really nice to talk and compare lives – 'Oh, that happened to me,' or 'Yes, I got that done as well.'

It was so cool. A whole room of bladder exstrophy people – and every one of us felt like we fitted in.

What made it even better was the fact one of the organisers had arranged a little area showing the latest equipment for people with our condition. So I actually ended up getting a new catheter while I was there. Imagine having my condition and finding a kind of market stall where you could go and try new equipment!

All of Mr Ransley's patients were in a great mood. A few people told him they were going to get their belly button pierced, just to see the look on his face when he heard that all his good work would be undone.

Mostly though, we all told Mr Ransley how very grateful we were for what he had done for us. There was a large commemorative book in which you could write a message for him. Every time I looked over at him his eyes seemed to be watering, and I'm sure he would have shed a few more tears when he got round to reading that.

But the evening didn't end there. After the party with the patients, Mr Ransley had another celebration with his colleagues and hospital staff. About five of us patients were invited along to surprise him. I was chosen, I think, because of all the public speaking I'd done before. They knew I wouldn't get nervous by having to say a few words in front of a large audience. One doctor also said that I had been one of Mr Ransley's sickest patients, so I think that might have had something to do with it as well.

We had to be smuggled in which was very funny. Every time Mr Ransley stood up, we had to dive behind a chair or hide under a table, which made everyone else laugh. I think Mr Ransley thought people were laughing at him! Eventually we all went on stage to talk about him and he rolled his eyes because he realised it was us who everyone had been laughing at.

Before Mr Ransley's retirement, the mother of one of his patients had tried to nominate him for royal recognition. She had organised for lots of former patients and staff and colleagues to write letters of recommendation, and although the campaign for recognition hadn't succeeded, she still had all the letters saying how many people's lives Mr Ransley had saved. So that evening, one little girl's mother went on stage and said, 'We've brought those letters here tonight so you can see what people think about you.' It was a wonderful moment and Mr Ransley was really moved by it. I think we all were.

I was privileged to be asked to thank him on behalf of all his patients. I don't think there was a dry eye in the room. I really struggled to finish my script but I don't think it would have mattered if I'd stopped. Everyone there had their own kind words and heartfelt thanks for the guest of honour. I was just lucky that I got to say mine in public. The more people I can tell about Mr Ransley's brilliance, the better.

I don't really know why the fundraising office at Great Ormond Street kept asking me to speak at events. There are millions of children around who owe the hospital their lives, and I'm sure there would be no shortage of volunteers to help out if they were asked. I guess they saw that I was quite comfortable on stage and that people seemed to like hearing my story. I don't really get nervous any more – not for myself, at least. Because I'm doing it for the hospital, I am conscious of not wanting to let them down, and that is the only thing that worries me before I go on. I have this huge fear of failure because of that. I always worry that if I make a mistake it will affect the amount of money we can raise for the hospital.

The fundraisers all tell me not to worry, to just be myself. They say that because I've done well in the past. But each event is different. And everyone has such high expectations of me.

One of the things I never get used to is seeing all those faces staring at me. I feel their eyes burning into me as I walk up to the microphone. Once I'm speaking, I dare not look at anybody's face. I concentrate and focus on one part of the wall at the back and hope that nobody catches my eye.

Of course, once my speech is over I can relax, let my hair down and enjoy myself.

In August 2005, I was invited to do something a little different. Dad and I caught the train down to London and then found our way to Harrods in Knightsbridge. I'd heard so much about this amazing shop but I'd never been before. I think my brothers saw it while I was in hospital. I missed out on so much when I was ill.

There were lots of celebrities there for the Diesel Fashion Show in aid of Great Ormond Street, and they all modelled clothes by walking up and down a long catwalk. For some reason I was asked to parade up and down as well! It was thoroughly nerve-wracking and I thought I would trip over at any moment.

At the end, the shop's owner, Mohamed Al Fayed, said I'd done a brilliant job and gave me a Harrods anniversary teddy bear as a reward.

By now, I was starting to enjoy myself a bit more. A few weeks later I was invited back to the Hotel de France in Jersey for that year's fundraising event. This time it was a 'Crystal Ball', but before I could enjoy that there was work to be done.

Because we'd got on so well the year before, Caroline Strachen invited Dad and me to stay at their house rather than in a hotel. It was great to see Catherine again, but the downside was that we couldn't just watch everyone running around setting up the event without mucking in ourselves!

There were only a few days to get everything done. It looked very fancy, with a giant crystal suspended above the stage and lots of smaller crystals decorating the walls and tables.

It must have been the hottest summer for years. I can still picture Dad sweating as he lugged all those chairs around.

Catherine and I were given hundreds of pens and a great big paper pad and told, 'We need these pens for tonight – keep scribbling till you find the ones that work.'

One of the other jobs we had was to count the tables. There should have been fifty, according to the number of tickets that had been sold, but it was really hard to keep track of where you'd counted to in such a large room. I checked and double-checked, then said to one of the organisers, 'Guys, I think there's a problem – there are only forty-nine tables.'

While the adults ran around looking for the missing furniture, I was given the job of tying balloons onto all the chairs. It didn't seem like hard work until I realised I'd only tied a dozen bows and my fingers were already beginning to get sore. I remember thinking, 'Why do the smallest details take the longest? Only another 500 to go . . .'

I had no idea we'd be working so hard when I agreed to speak there. But at least Catherine and I did get first taste of the chocolate fountain!

Eventually the hotel ballroom was ready, and the event got under way. I met Rula Lenska, author Jack Higgins, John Nettles who used to play Bergerac in the TV series and John Altman – 'Nasty' Nick Cotton from EastEnders. After all the effort we'd put in during the day, Catherine and I had a great time letting off steam by running around the ballroom. It made such a change not to spend every minute worrying about my speech, as I would normally have been at that point. Then I lost track of Catherine, and asked Dad to help me look for her. He happened to be talking to John Altman at the time who offered to help as well. It was completely surreal seeing Nick Cotton being so nice! I heard him say to Dad, 'We look like a couple of cops.' Little did he know.

Whenever we attended an event like this I always wondered how on earth the hospital made any money from it. Everything looked so expensive. Sarah and the other fundraisers explained that lots of people donated gifts to the events and that everyone who came had to buy a ticket. So although it was expensive to host a function, they made a lot more money from each one than they spent. If there was a charity auction as well then just one event could make more than £100,000 for Great Ormond Street. I felt so honoured to be helping out.

In 2006, I was invited to appear at two very different fundraising events, but both with the same theme: pirates.

In May, Dad, my brother Martin and I flew over to Majorca to watch the opening night of production called Pirates Show which was about to start its summer season. Poor Kenneth couldn't come because he was doing his standard exams, and Mum refused to leave him on his own. Martin loved the fact that we got to party while our brother was studying!

Pirates Show is a big deal in Majorca. It has a massive set, a large cast and plays to thousands of holidaymakers throughout the summer. Every year the organisers host a charity dinner première to launch the show, and they invite nine families from Great Ormond Street to visit for the week. We were lucky enough to be one of them.

Because it was all in aid of the hospital, there were plenty of celebrities at the première, among them more sports personalities than I had ever seen. Linford Christie was there and Sally Gunnell, John Fashanu and Nigel Benn. The people I instantly recognised, though, were Angela Griffin, who is in *Holby City* and *Coronation Street*, and Steve McFadden – Phil from *EastEnders*. The weather girl Sian Lloyd was also there with her then boyfriend, politician Lembit Opik.

During the dinner Dad really embarrassed himself. He was convinced that one of the lead actors in the show – Aaron – looked just like George Best in his younger days, so he kept calling him that for the first couple of days that we were there. He would say things like, 'How are you getting on, Georgie Best?' It was only after the dinner that he realised that Alex Best – George Best's ex-wife – was there. She laughed, but I've never seen Dad go so red.

It was great seeing so many patients from Great Ormond Street and all our families got on very well. I made some close friends that week.

Everyone had different conditions – from heart trouble to cystic fibrosis, and many others besides – so it was really interesting for us to share our experiences with each other, and to learn more about other areas of the hospital that we hadn't got to see. It probably sounds odd to other people, but to us it just added to what was already such a fun week. Nobody was telling any of us that we couldn't join in because we were unwell; no one was saying, 'You just sit and watch.' Everyone took part in everything.

Pirates Show was so good that we all went a second time at the end of the week. When the cast found out we were there, they invited us all up onto the stage. No one had expected that. They made sure that everyone in the audience knew what a brilliant job Great Ormond Street does, and everyone clapped and cheered, which made us feel great.

The pirate theme continued with the publication of a new *Peter Pan* book in October. The income Great Ormond Street received from the original book was about to stop because the rights were reverting to the public domain. So the hospital had asked the writer Geraldine McCaughrean to create an official sequel. The launch for *Peter Pan in Scarlet* was held at Kensington Palace – it was a really glitzy affair with lots of champagne and some very well-dressed people. I was wearing a lovely red dress that Mum had bought for me for the occasion.

A little ten-year-old girl called Scarlett Saunders, who, like me, owed her life to Great Ormond Street, went up to collect a special leather-bound copy of the book (one of only five made) on behalf of the hospital. Then it was my turn to go up and give my speech.

I'd noticed when we arrived that there were lots of television cameras in place, which made me a little anxious. But Sarah from GOSH had told me not to worry. 'They're filming a documentary about Great Ormond Street,' she explained. 'Just give your speech as normal.'

I introduced myself: 'Ladies and gentlemen, my name is Kirsteen Lupton and I am a patient at Great Ormond Street Hospital,' I began. And, as soon as I started to speak, my nerves disappeared.

Afterwards Sarah congratulated me on my performance. We then got talking about various things, including famous people. I remember at one point she asked me if I liked Madonna. 'Oh no,' I said. 'Mum and Dad say she's an old slapper!' From the look on Sarah's face you would have thought Madonna was standing in the room! We laughed about that a lot; then I thought nothing further of it. Sarah pointed out to me some of the famous people who were there, including Sir Trevor Nunn, Andrew Sachs, George Layton and Lizo Mzimba, although I must admit I didn't really know who they all were before we were introduced. However, there was one famous face I really should have recognised, but didn't – not without his make-up, anyway.

A man approached us and as soon as I saw him I thought he looked familiar. 'My name's Jason Isaacs,' he said. 'You've just embarrassed me in front of everyone – I was in tears listening to you speak!'

The name Jason Isaacs is unforgettable to anyone who is a fan of the *Harry Potter* films. I've got them all on DVD and I watch them over and over again. The books are brilliant too. The really embarrassing thing for me, though, was that I couldn't remember which character Jason played! I've seen his name on the film credits so many times but I just couldn't place the face.

I was terrified that he would ask me if I knew who he was; but he was too nice for that. He didn't put me on the spot at all. We just sat and chatted about my experiences at the hospital, and about how impressed he had been with the way I spoke about all I had been through. Then he asked, 'Are you a fan of *Harry Potter*?'

I couldn't answer quickly enough.

'I'm doing some filming for the next *Harry Potter* film next week,' he said. 'Would you be interested in coming to the set to see what goes on?'

I couldn't believe what I was hearing. I never gave speeches to get anything out of it, but I wasn't about to turn down an offer like this one.

We chatted for a while longer and I could barely contain my excitement. As soon as Jason was out of earshot I rushed over to Sarah and asked her who his character was in the *Harry Potter* films.

'I don't blame you for not recognising him,' Sarah said. 'He's not wearing his Lucius Malfoy wig.'

Malfoy! The most evil – well, second-most evil – man in the world of *Harry Potter* had just been so nice to me. Who would have thought? No wonder I couldn't place him.

The Order of the Phoenix was being shot in Leavesden, in the south of England. Getting there from Glasgow wouldn't be the easiest trip but there was no way in the world I wanted to pass up this opportunity.

The night before we were due on set, Dad, Kenneth, Martin and I drove down to stay with my dad's parents in Liverpool so that we wouldn't have too much of a journey the next day. It was really nice seeing them again and being able to spend some time with them.

While we were there, my dad got a phone call. I immediately knew it was from Jason, and, from the look on Dad's face, I could tell it was bad news.

I could barely bring myself to listen to the conversation.

'OK, Jason. I understand,' Dad said. 'Are you sure?'

My heart sank. He was pulling out. I knew the offer had been too good to be true. I braced myself.

But then I heard, 'OK, Jason. We'll see you tomorrow.'

I can't describe my relief at that moment. I think I almost stopped breathing during their conversation.

Jason had phoned, in fact, to warn us that there had been a change of plan and that he wouldn't be filmed the next day. Like me, Dad had assumed this meant our visit was being cancelled. Far from it.

'Don't worry, I'm still coming to show you around,' Jason

had told him. 'I just didn't want Kirsteen to be disappointed that she wouldn't see me acting.'

I was amazed. Jason lives about two and a half hours away from the set, yet he was still prepared to drive out on his day off just to give us a guided tour.

I was so excited that night I could barely sleep. Martin and I chatted about the films for the whole journey down from Liverpool, and when we arrived at the Leavesden studios Jason was ready and waiting for us. He took us everywhere, and I actually saw some of the scenes being filmed. I met a lot of the other actors too, and although I didn't get to see Jason in his incredible blond Lucius wig, those four hours were easily the best of my life.

It was hard to believe that I'd been so lucky just because I had been trying to help Great Ormond Street. And, little did I know, my luck was not about to end there.

CHAPTER 14

Isn't He a Bit Gorgeous?

KIRSTEEN: Lying in bed in Yorkhill I could never have dreamed that one day I would meet celebrities and visit film studios. Even once I had been cured by Great Ormond Street I didn't expect that.

Nobody can predict the future. Not least Mum and Dad – they certainly never thought they would give birth to a baby with bladder exstrophy. And I could not possibly have imagined what happened to me in 2006.

I'd been told I was going to be filmed for a documentary about children who had been in hospital. I thought they were going to ask me about where I'd been treated, what was wrong with me, how I'd got better. Things like that. Dad told me I'd have to go down to London again. 'It's going to be a whole day's filming,' he said, 'although they'll probably only use a couple of minutes.'

I wasn't exactly thrilled at the idea. For a start it seemed so vain. I'm happy to talk about the hospital to anyone who will listen. It's another story, though, when someone just wants to talk about me. And the idea of travelling so far just to do that didn't appeal at all. But after a few days, Dad managed to persuade me to take part and so, once again, we made the journey down to the hospital.

In the end, I was glad I did because as soon as we got there I bumped into Dr Jane Collins, Chief Executive of Great Ormond Street; I always liked speaking to her. We had a chat, and then she said, 'I hear you've won a big award.'

Then Dad appeared, seemingly out of nowhere, and whisked me away, saying, 'Big award? Our Kirsteen? No, you must have got the wrong person there.'

I was so tired from the long journey that I thought nothing further of it.

Later that day, I was told that GMTV wanted to interview me the next morning about the documentary for their television review section. I wasn't really sure what I could say to them but, as usual, I welcomed the opportunity to tell the world about Great Ormond Street.

The next morning, Dad and I were up at the crack of dawn, ready to be driven to the studio, where we were met by the presenter Kate Garroway during a commercial break. She made us feel at home, then I was shown over to the sofa and, suddenly, the cameras were all pointing my way. Kate asked me lots of questions about my fundraising and I couldn't really see where it was going. I was wondering where the man who was meant to be doing the documentary was when Kate handed me a large gold envelope, and said, 'This is for you.'

I was so confused. What on earth was it?

Then, as I opened it, she said, 'Congratulations. You've just won a Pride of Britain award.'

I was completely shocked; I hadn't been expecting anything like this. I was speechless – I don't think it made for great live television.

'How do you feel?' Kate asked.

It all seemed too much. My mouth felt very dry, and I just about managed to say, 'I don't know. It hasn't sunk in yet.'

I've never seen a video of that interview, and I don't think I ever want to. Afterwards I got a text from a friend who said, 'You looked really excited – *not!*'

As Dad and I drove away in a taxi, I examined the contents of the envelope more closely and saw the invitation to the awards ceremony to be held in London a few weeks later.

'Well,' said Dad, 'what do you think?'

I still didn't know what to say. All I could do was smile.

MARTIN: The wheels had been set in motion for that little surprise some months earlier.

Once Kirsteen began appearing at charity functions, I got quite used to receiving letters and telephone calls from people asking to interview her or enquiring as to whether she would be available to attend various events. Then, in the summer of 2006 I received a call from another 'unknown' number and assumed it would be of a similar nature. And it was – but I had no idea where it would lead.

The caller introduced herself to me, explaining that she was working for a company who were making a documentary about sixteen people who had done special things with their lives. She said she'd read about Kirsteen's charity appearances in the press and thought she might make a good subject.

'Do you think you could send me some details about Kirsteen?' she asked. 'Just a brief synopsis of her achievements and of what she went through when she was a baby.'

I did as she requested and then forgot all about the call. It wasn't out of the ordinary to be asked for things like that, and what with trying to hold down a full-time job with overtime, and keep up with three teenage children, things do sometimes just slip off your radar.

But then a few days later she called again. She'd been impressed by the outline of Kirsteen's life, but told me she had a confession to make. 'We're not just making a documentary about special people,' she said. 'I actually work for the Pride of Britain awards – and we're delighted to tell you that your daughter has won the Fundraiser of the Year award.'

I was stunned.

She went on to give me some more details but I already knew a lot about the awards. They were started in 1999 by the *Daily Mirror* newspaper to celebrate the 'real' people who had done tremendous things in that year and they had a very well-deserved reputation as the most uplifting awards in the world. The first ceremony was hosted by Carol Vorderman, and held at the Dorchester Hotel in London's Park Lane. Among the winners that first year was Donna Marie McGillion, who had narrowly survived the Omagh bomb a year earlier. And even though they weren't there to accept any awards – and there were no television cameras! – people like Tony Blair, Sir Paul McCartney, Victoria Beckham and Queen Noor of Jordan all turned up to pay tribute to the winners. The awards drew so much publicity that I wasn't surprised when the ceremony was televised the following year.

Jill is a big fan of anything like that and I don't think we've missed a single show since the awards started; to think that our Kirsteen was being honoured in this way was just incredible.

Some amazing stories have been told on Pride of Britain over the years – little children who have saved their brothers and sisters from house fires, people who have risked their lives to rescue the elderly, servicemen who regularly put others' safety before their own as part of their day-to-day work – and every single winner has been thoroughly deserving of their accolade. The fact that 10 million viewers tune in to the awards, and that they attract people like HRH Prince Charles, Gordon Brown, David Beckham, Bono, President Bill Clinton, Dame Helen Mirren, Sir Richard Branson, Kylie Minogue and Robbie Williams, is a testament to just how well respected they are.

When I thought about it, I could see why Kirsteen had been chosen. She had gone through an awful lot as a wee girl, although lots of children have suffered like her, and many, like young Alex, were not as fortunate. But what had really caught the imagination of the awards' organisers was the fact that she was so happy to use her spare time to raise both money and awareness for the hospital that had saved her.

It's impossible to express just how proud I felt. It's one thing that Jill and I and Kirsteen's brothers think she is incredible; it's an entirely different thing when a total stranger calls up to tell say that they agree.

It was actually, as we learned, the fundraising department of the GOSH Children's Charity (GOSHCC) that put Kirsteen forward for the award. Clare Cook, who had organised the Grand Prix Ball, nominated her for consideration by a panel of judges that included Dame Kelly Holmes, Sharon and Ozzy Osbourne, among others. She told me, 'I was so blown away by the effect Kirsteen had on our fundraising that night that I thought she deserved some recognition. So many people are very grateful to her.'

But what she said next staggered me. 'According to our calculations Kirsteen has helped to raise more than £700,000. If anyone deserves the award of Fundraiser of the Year it's her.'

Of course, I was bursting to tell Jill – but there was one person who couldn't find out.

Kirsteen.

It would have been hard enough if we could have just forgotten about it until November, but the organisers needed our help several times before then.

The first thing they wanted was some footage of Kirsteen giving one of her speeches. I told them that she would be appearing at the GOSH event to launch the *Peter Pan* sequel. 'That's perfect,' they said. 'We'll just let everyone know we're making a documentary about the hospital and no one will suspect anything.'

They also wanted to film Kirsteen being told about the award live on GMTV later in the year, so plans had to be made to get her there without raising suspicion.

The third thing was more complicated. To make it a night that Kirsteen would never ever forget, they wanted to find a favourite celebrity who would be asked to present her trophy.

'She'd be very happy to see Cat Deeley,' I said.

But they were thinking bigger than that. 'It has to be someone really high profile,' they told me. 'We're thinking film stars. Someone like Johnny Depp.'

I gasped. Kirsteen would faint if she met him, I thought. 'Johnny Depp might fit the bill,' I said.

We chatted for a while longer about other possibilities, then the producer said, 'We're hoping to spring a surprise on Kirsteen during her speech at Kensington Palace. Don't be surprised if someone like Madonna comes out of the woodwork!'

I don't know how far efforts to engage Madonna's services ever got, but a few weeks later I cringed when I overheard Kirsteen's response to Sarah's question as to whether she liked Madonna! I thought I would die of embarrassment.

More embarrassing still, however, was a phone call a few days later. One of the production team called me, very excited, and said, 'You know we promised you a movie star? Well, we've managed to get Jude Law to present Kirsteen's award.'

To which I, to my eternal shame, said, 'Oh great – who's she?'

KIRSTEEN: I never had any goal in mind when I started raising money for Great Ormond Street. I didn't really know how it all worked. I just knew I wanted to help. The most I thought I would ever make for the hospital was about £500 – although when my autograph sold for so much at the Grand Prix Ball I had to adjust my expectations a little bit.

So when I heard that I had helped to raise three-quarters of a million pounds I was astounded. I knew I'd been doing it for years, and I knew each event was really successful, but I'd never once thought about how all the funds added together. Each function was a one-off event for the hospital as far as I was concerned. And it was never about me. That wasn't the reason I was doing it. I just couldn't believe that anybody had been so generous as to think about me when they had so many other things to worry about.

As usual, Dad went to see my teachers and asked for permission for me to miss classes. I don't know if it's because of what I've been through or the fact that I'm raising money for charity, but the school has always supported my days off in term time. It's another reason why some of my friends are jealous of me – not only do I get to meet celebrities, but I get to do it in school time. I think I would be envious of me as well!

The night we arrived in London there was a big dinner at the City Inn Hotel in Westminster. All the organisers and the GOSH team were there. Carol Vorderman, the host of the event, came over to speak to us. She was lovely and made me feel really comfortable, even though I knew that millions of people would be watching the programme. She explained what would be happening, so that I wouldn't be confused; I was really impressed that she took the time to make sure we were OK, as I was sure she could have asked someone else to do all that for her.

The next day we were all bussed over to the ITV studios for a rehearsal in the afternoon. We had to hang around for quite a bit while they went through all the technical preparations. That just made my nerves worse. I suddenly realised that I was more worried about this than when I had to give a speech. At least then I had something to take my mind off things. This time it wouldn't be my words that were the centre of attention. It would be me. I really wasn't looking forward to that.

I've seen a lot of celebrities in my life but I'd never seen so many in one room as when the actual awards ceremony began. I was so pleased that Mum and my brothers had come down for this. I've experienced a lot of nice things through my work for GOSH, and I was really happy that they could share in this one as well.

Although Mum doesn't usually come with me to events as she doesn't like to leave my brothers, she and I get to enjoy the experience in a different way. Whenever there is a function coming up she takes me for a girls' day out and we go round all the shops looking at different outfits, shoes and make-up. Then she takes me to get my hair done and sits there waiting until I'm ready to go home. When I actually get on stage to present my speeches, Dad usually calls Mum and leaves the phone open so she can hear every word.

But this time it was different. At the Pride of Britain awards Mum could finally see me in person.

All the award winners and presenters and special guests were seated around giant round tables in front of the stage. There were only enough chairs for me, Mum and Dad, so Kenneth and Martin watched from a large gallery on the floor above. I think they had a great time. Every time I looked up they were pointing to another famous person. We could see Tony and Cherie Blair, Girls Aloud, Noel Edmonds, Take That, Kelly Brook, Sharon Osbourne, Emma Bunton, Gary Lineker, Dame Kelly Holmes, the cast of The Bill. It was really intimidating to think that I would soon be getting up in front of all these famous people.

But the moment had arrived. One of the television people appeared at our table and said it was time. I was really nervous as I heard Carol Vorderman begin her introduction. 'Our next winner is the Fundraiser of the Year and, frankly, we're lucky to have her here. As you'll see, she's a very busy woman.' On a large screen behind her were pictures of me from when I was in Yorkhill with my legs in plaster, then later at Great Ormond Street. They showed various scenes of me appearing at events that Dad had filmed. Then I noticed footage of me giving my speech at the launch of *Peter Pan in Scarlet*. I'd never seen that before.

That was when the penny dropped. So that was why the television cameras were there, I realised.

The next thing I saw was Dad's video of my autograph being auctioned. I couldn't believe how young I looked. An interview with Clare Cook was being played as a soundtrack over the video: 'It was a huge room with thousands of people and Kirsteen went up there by herself, a tiny figure in a little white dress, and spoke with such emotion that there was a tear in everyone's eye. It was one of the most amazing moments of my life.'

Then the screen went blank. I braced myself.

Carol called my name and I knew that this was it. Come on, you can do it, I told myself as I got up from our table and walked out into the spotlight.

I was nearly knocked out by the glare. I've been on stage lots of times, but this was dazzling – like being out in the sun at midday.

Carol put me right at ease immediately. 'You look stunning,' she told me, then explained to the audience how ill I had been, how Great Ormond Street had saved my life and how I had raised £700,000 for them, including the time I had auctioned my signature for so much money. 'You're doing an excellent job,' she said. 'Almost a million pounds so far and hopefully you'll hit that million soon. It's wonderful to see you looking so well – you're a great advertisement for Great Ormond Street.'

She told me that because I'd already met so many celebrities they had struggled to find someone suitable to present my award. 'But I think we've done it. Please welcome Britain's most successful young actor, Oscar nominee and a dad – Jude Law.'

I'm embarrassed to admit that although I knew his name, I'd never seen any of his films. But as soon as he stepped out I recognised him. He had just done a film called The Holiday with Cameron Diaz, and had been in every newspaper for weeks.

Jude Law was lovely. He gave me a kiss on each cheek and a great big hug. He was really funny as well. 'I sold my autograph last week and it raised £3.50,' he said. 'Then they found out it included a free photograph and it made £2.50.'

I laughed so much that my knees finally stopped knocking. But what he said next made me feel faint.

'Kirsteen, I'm absolutely bowled over to meet you. To recover with such inner strength and to use that strength to raise this money is an extraordinary achievement. What I do is so easy. I get given lines and I learn them and deliver them. But to write speeches and speak from the heart and move people in that way is a truly unique skill and I'm so proud to be able to give you this award.'

All I could manage to say was, 'Thank you.'

Carol could see I was tongue-tied, so she said, 'Isn't he a bit gorgeous?'

Then I said, 'He's OK,' and made everyone in the room laugh.

It was incredible to be up there with a famous TV star and a Hollywood actor. Obviously, since that night I've learned what a massive star Jude Law is and how often he wins Best-looking Man competitions. I'm sure when I'm a bit older I'll look back and wish I could meet him again!

I was then presented with the award, which is really heavy because it's platinum-coated. And just when I thought I could leave, Carol said, 'The night's not over for you, young lady. We've got an extra surprise.' I had no idea what was going to happen next. I'd already received my award. What more could there be?

'Now, I know that you love them,' Carol said, 'and they've got a little pressie for you. McFly!'

My favourite band. And there they all were, Tom, Dougie, Harry and Danny, running onto the stage to see me!

They all gave me a kiss and then Carol said, 'Isn't she amazing?'

'Absolutely,' said Danny.

'Incredible,' Tom agreed. Then he noticed me looking at the guitar he was holding. 'We know how hard it is to raise money and we thought we'd try to help you out a bit,' he said. 'So we're giving you one of our guitars which we've all signed. Hopefully you can auction it and raise a bit of money.'

Then they all stood back and started to clap me.

It all happened so fast it was like a dream. I was too stunned to speak or even move. I was so embarrassed by all the attention. Jude Law came over and put his arm round me and helped me off stage where I got to chat with McFly for longer. I have no idea what I said. I've never been star-struck before, but I think I might have been then.

After the programme finished recording, lots of people came over to our table to say how moved they were to hear my story and to congratulate me for all the money I'd raised.

Tony and Cherie Blair were the first to come across. I never thought I'd have a Prime Minister asking to speak to me! They were so nice that even Mum was moved. She's been a member of the Conservative Party all her life, so I think she was disappointed by how much she liked them!

The *X-Factor* judges all came over as well and I had my photograph taken with them. Simon wasn't as scary as he is on television and Sharon was as nice as you'd expect. Mum even got her to speak to one of my friends, Katy Anderson, on the phone, which was hilarious. I don't think she believed it was really Sharon.

Afterwards, there was a party held in a giant marquee where we met even more people. My brothers couldn't understand why I wasn't gob-smacked at seeing all the celebrities. Martin was wandering around open-mouthed, saying, 'Oh my God, that's David Hasselhoff' or 'I can't believe Tony Blair just came to speak to you.' And even Kenneth was a bit shocked. 'How can you not be impressed by this?' he asked.

I've thought about that question a lot and I think that part of the reason was that I had met so many celebrities by that stage that it wasn't a new experience for me. I was just as impressed as my brothers were but not in an awestruck kind of way. I was actually blown away by how nice and generous everyone was, and I think that's more important to me. Because of what I've been through in my own life I don't like to treat anyone as 'different'. Regardless of whether they look different, they have a famous name or they've done impressive things, they're all still people, and I don't believe that any one person is better (or worse) than another just because of who he is. And I certainly don't believe that I'm a better person now I've raised so much money than when I was being pushed around town in a wheelchair and children were staring at me.

KENNETH: When Kirsteen got the Pride of Britain award it was really nice for us to get a glimpse of what she does on a regular basis. It was fantastic. I don't ever feel jealous – well, maybe just a bit when my brother gets to go off on trips with her as well. But seeing the Prime Minister come up to her like she was a long-lost friend was pretty mind-blowing. Most people would have turned to jelly but she just took it in her stride. There were so many celebrities in the room and they all seemed to be queuing up to meet her – and this was all after the television cameras had stopped rolling. No one was doing it just to be seen.

MARTIN JR: A lot of my friends say I must be jealous of Kirsteen because of all the celebrities she gets to meet and all the cool parties she's invited to. They seem fascinated by it all; someone once even 'Googled' her name while I was with him and read things out about her condition as if I knew nothing about it. I think he was just trying to shock me, but that's ridiculous. Sometimes it takes a while to make other people see that Kirsteen's a normal girl who just happens to have been ill when she was small, and who now gets to meet lots famous actors and pop stars through her fundraising work.

I have mixed feelings about all the celebrity parties. I've gone along with Kirsteen a few times and I've met plenty of famous people, but she's the one who deserves all the attention. She's the one who's been through all the pain, she's the one who's raised all that money for charity, so it's only right that she gets some sort of 'upside' too. When I go to one of her events, I'm just happy to stay in the background and watch her talk to everyone. It's just nice to see my sister happy.

The only person who really made an impression on me was Jason Isaacs because he went so far out of his way to be nice to Kirsteen and to all of us. It was really decent of him to take the time to do that, especially as he wasn't even working that day. I guess he was really impressed by Kirsteen. And for me it was so exciting to be taken around the *Harry Potter* set that it actually inspired me to take up acting.

KIRSTEEN: On the day of the Pride of Britain awards I was interviewed by Channel Five news, as well as by lots of newspaper journalists. But that wasn't all.

All of the winners were invited to tea at Number 10, Downing Street the following morning. Who would have thought that I would walk through that famous door and be greeted by the Prime Minister and his wife. It was a great gesture on their part.

The whole Pride of Britain experience really changed my life. Everywhere I went people were so nice to me. I think it even improved things for me at school because all those who had been a bit critical when I started meeting people like Cat Deeley now saw the reason why I was doing it. Within an hour of appearing on GMTV I had received about fifty texts from people saying things like, 'Oh my God, I just saw you on television!' The weird thing was that most of the messages were from numbers I didn't even recognise. When I spoke to my best friend Katie Angus, she told me that everyone at school was talking about it.

When I returned to school I could hear people talking about me and who I'd met, but this time nobody resented me for it. They'd all seen what I'd been through in my life and I don't think anyone would have wanted to swap places with me. No celebrity can make up for all those years of suffering.

CHAPTER 15

The Great and the Good

KIRSTEEN: Winning a Pride of Britain award meant more to me than anyone can ever know. Not because I got to meet all those great people – although I admit I really enjoyed all of that – but because for every moment I was on television, Great Ormond Street Hospital was being seen by millions of television viewers. And if every one of those viewers donated just one pound to the charity, that would be an incredible sum.

It was the perfect event I thought when I got home. I'd had a great time, as had all the guests and celebrities, lots of charities got tons of exposure and millions of people watching television enjoyed a very entertaining programme. Everyone must be happy.

I had no idea that some people wouldn't be happy with

the Pride of Britain awards at all. And the thing that annoyed them the most was me.

Mum discovered it first. Now we are all at school and my health is so much better she does part-time work in a supermarket. She was there one day when one of the doctors from Yorkhill came in. He was paying for his shopping when a lady said to him, 'Did you see young Kirsteen on the television this week?'

'I did,' he replied.

'Don't you think it's fantastic how she's raised all this money for that children's hospital?' the lady said.

'No! I think it's disgusting.' Apparently he was really angry. 'She should be doing it for Yorkhill – not some English hospital.'

When the lady saw Mum a few minutes later she told her every word. 'If he comes back in this store he'll know all about it,' Mum said.

People have even said similar things to me. They're so narrow-minded they cannot get their heads around the fact that Great Ormond Street is a British hospital for British children. When I was in there I met Scottish people, Irish people and English people. Everyone was treated exactly the same. And we all have one thing in common: we all owe the hospital our quality of life – if not our lives.

Why wouldn't I want to help the people who helped me? I always try to explain to people that I haven't made a random decision. Great Ormond Street was able to help me and Yorkhill wasn't. I can't be any more diplomatic than that. But they only see it as 'Scottish versus English'. To be honest, it makes me ashamed to be Scottish sometimes, but I know if their children were in trouble they'd all want to do the best for them. When my GP referred me to London he said, 'If it was my daughter I would do the same.' Until it happens to them I think people shouldn't judge.

Thanks to Great Ormond Street, no one would ever know there's anything wrong with me today. To be honest, I don't think I could ever be any better, and I consider myself very lucky. There are so many other people who have medical problems that *can't* be helped.

Still, I can't say that my condition never gets me down, because it does. I remember once, when I was eleven, I got so frustrated at not being able to do PE at school with everyone else that it actually made me cry. Normally I wouldn't have let my feelings get the better of me, but when I came home I wrote a note and put it under Mum's pillow on my way up to bed.

It read: 'I hate bladder exstrophy.'

I don't know what I was trying to achieve. All I knew then was that I was upset that day and needed to tell someone. Days like that do come along occasionally.

People think I'm cured but I'm not. What I am is 'better', although compared to how I was a few years ago, I can hardly recognise myself.

I'll have to drain for the rest of my life and I really do hate it. The fact that I can only go about four hours between each drain is annoying. It means that Mum and Dad don't like me going out into town with my friends unless I carry a catheter with me, even if I say I'll be back in time. This is the thing I argue about with them the most. If I do go out for the day, they virtually stand over me to make sure I drain before I go out, and then they phone to remind me to drain later. They don't have to bother though. If my bladder gets too full it actually hurts, so there is no way I could forget – the pain would be too unbearable.

My parents watch me like a hawk even when I'm at home. If I've got friends over and I'm due to drain Mum yells up, 'Kirsteen, have you had your medicine yet?'

I'll usually say something like, 'Not yet, Mum. In a few minutes.'

And she will demand, 'No, Kirsteen. Now!'

I always try to get away with it for as long as I can. I know it does me no good, but I think I just need to prove to myself that I'm in charge. I hate the idea of being beaten by my condition.

I still have to go down to Great Ormond Street for annual check-ups, and when I turn sixteen I'll be transferred to the Middlesex Hospital, which specialises in the same problem in adults.

I guess I think of myself as a positive person. I try to look on the bright side and I know I'm lucky to be alive. But I do have my down moments, like anyone, and I really wish I could be 'normal'. The doctors are really happy with my progress, although there are no guarantees that I'll ever be able to have children.

But I don't like to dwell on negative things. I'd rather enjoy my life as much as possible. I've got my school, my friends and home, and I like to leave it at that for now. Maybe I'm being naïve, though. Maybe I'm just bottling everything up, and one day, when I sit down and reflect on it all, I'll just break down and it will all pour out of me.

But at the moment I'm OK with it.

Last time I was in hospital Mr Mushtaq asked me what I wanted to do when I grow up.

'I want to work in medicine,' I replied.

I could tell he was shocked. 'Really? Haven't you seen enough of the insides of hospitals?'

According to Mr Mushtaq, virtually nobody who has experienced major operations ever wants to practise medicine. But I feel that I could be useful *because* of my experiences. If I had a patient who was upset I think it would help so much if I could reassure them and say, 'Don't worry – I've been through it myself. You will get better. Look at me.' It always made such a difference to me when I met people who had been through surgery and had built normal lives. Inya Wallace is my favourite example.

My whole family has been affected by my experiences in one way or another. Kenneth still says he loves the atmosphere in hospitals because he remembers how wonderful it was at Great Ormond Street. And, like me, he also now wants to study medicine.

Every Saturday he does a wonderful thing, volunteering at a local club run for people with learning difficulties. He helps out there with some of the boys and girls who range in age from five to twenty-five, talking to them, feeding them and entertaining them.

My brother Martin is just as caring. He has a friend with very bad cerebral palsy who comes over to our house and stays the night. Martin's wonderful with him, whereas other kids don't take an interest because he's disabled. As far as they're concerned, it's sad, but it's not their problem. We're not like that in our family. We know what it's like to be the 'problem'.

I'm really proud to belong to a family who would do anything for anyone who needed help, whether they were a friend or a stranger.

At the end of 2007 though, it was someone much closer to home who needed help.

It came out of nowhere. We were all sitting round the dining table one day when Mum announced, 'I don't want to worry you but I have to go into hospital for a triple heart bypass.'

It was typical of Mum. She likes to rant and rave, but when it's come to something big, she's the calmest person in the world. She explained that she'd been feeling a bit run-down, so she'd gone to the doctor and he'd run some tests and found that she would need major surgery.

It didn't help that just two days before Mum found out she would have to undergo this operation, her own mother had died. They'd never seen eye to eye, but somehow Mum still ended up having to sort out most of the funeral arrangements.

But Mum seemed to take everything in her stride. I remember asking her just before the operation how she could be so calm. She answered simply that there was nothing she could do about it.

I saw Mum just before she was taken down to theatre and she looked fine, walking about as normal. So I was totally unprepared for what she'd look like a few hours later. She looked so ill, wired up to machines and covered with tubes. It really brought home to me how it must have been for my family when they came to visit me after my operations. But at least it meant that I knew how Mum felt; I knew she was pleased to see us but didn't have the energy to respond. I knew she was happy just knowing we were there.

And the fact that I'd been through so much myself actually gave me confidence that Mum would be OK. I wanted to stay as positive for her as she had been for me all my life.

One thing that keeps me smiling today is hearing about the efforts other people make to help Great Ormond Street. When I see people like Sir Alan Sugar donate a lot of their time and money it makes me want to carry on doing as much as I can. And when I heard that Johnny Depp was so grateful to the hospital for treating his little girl that he turned up there one day dressed completely in his Jack Sparrow costume (from *Pirates of the Caribbean*), I nearly wished I was ill again, just so I could have seen it. Nearly, but not quite!

I feel the best I can do now is to be there when the phone rings with fundraising requests.

Not long ago, I was back in London for another extravaganza. When I asked one of the organisers what the theme was, they told me it was a gathering of 'the great and the good'. They were referring to celebrities like Ruby Wax, Vernon Kay, Claudia Winkleman and Nick Knowles who would all be attending. But on the night, when I looked around at all the other people who had bought tickets to support the hospital, I thought: everyone here is great and good.

Of course, the real heroes are the people who actually work at the hospital. They do such incredible things and they all seem to care personally about each and every patient.

I was so proud to have been asked to speak at Mr Ransley's retirement party. And I'm also really happy that I've stayed in touch, to this day, with quite a few of the people I met during my time in London. Two of the nurses, Marika and Evelyn, have been up to stay with us a few times and we were all invited to Marika's wedding in September 2004.

I think it's no coincidence that I keep meeting such wonderful people through my connection with Great Ormond Street. It is a unique institution and I owe it my life. And for every day now that I wake up with a smile instead of a grimace of pain, I will never ever forget it.

Acknowledgements

Kirsteen and her family would like to thank sincerely all the professional and wonderful staff at Great Ormond Street Hospital for Children who have worked wonders in giving her the quality of life she enjoys today. Particular thanks to the staff of the Urodynamics department, under the expert guidance of Sister Brid Carr, and the staff on the Louise Ward in the autumn of 2000. A very special thanks to staff nurses Evelyn Douglas and Marika Clow (now Havers) who were not only the most dedicated of carers during Kirsteen's worst times, but who also became very special friends.

We would also like to thank all the dedicated staff of the Great Ormond Street Hospital Charity for their continuing monumental efforts in raising the funds to maintain and indeed improve the national institution that we and countless others have come to know and love, and to which we owe everything. Thanks especially to Clare Cook, who was kind enough to nominate Kirsteen – successfully – for the Pride of Britain award, which was the culmination of a whirlwind of wonderful experiences.

Thanks to Jane Wallace, chairperson of BEES, who encouraged us to go to Great Ormond Street in the first place.

Huge thanks, of course, to the anonymous donor who bid £20,000 for Kirsteen's autograph at Silverstone in 2004, giving her fundraising campaign the most fantastic foundation!

Thanks to all the great and the good whom we have met in the course of attending Kirsteen's events. You have given so generously of your time and endeavours. Mr Jason Isaacs . . . you were 'simply the best' for taking us round the *Harry Potter* set, and we think that you deserve the title role one day in your own James Bond film!

Thanks to the friends and those of our family who have stuck by us through the years, to Dot Clark who looked after Kirsteen all the way through pre- and primary school and to Hamish and Lloydette for their support in the role of surrogate grandparents.

We'd like to make a very special mention of little Alex Harrington who sadly didn't make it. You are never far from our thoughts, Alex, and you were such a brave fighter.

The biggest thanks of all are reserved for our very own superhero Mr Philip Ransley MA MB Bchir FRCS FAAP (Hon.) and his surgical team, including Mr Imran Mushtaq (now Mr Ransley's replacement as Kirsteen's urology consultant), who performed such surgical wizardry in 2000 – Harry Potter eat your heart out!